The
Consequences
of
Ideas

Understanding the Concepts

That Shaped Our World

R. C. SPROUL

CROSSWAY BOOKS • WHEATON, ILLINOIS
A DIVISION OF GOOD NEWS PUBLISHERS

The Consequences of Ideas

Copyright © 2000 by R. C. Sproul

Published by Crossway Books
        a division of Good News Publishers
        1300 Crescent Street
        Wheaton, Illinois 60187

Cover design: Cindy Kiple

First printing 2000

Printed in the United States of America

Unless marked otherwise, Scripture references are from the *New King James Version.* Copyright © 1982, Thomas Nelson, Inc. Used by permission.

The Scripture reference marked KJV is from the King James Version.

Library of Congress Cataloging-in-Publication Data
Sproul, R. C. (Robert Charles), 1939-
  The consequences of ideas : understanding the concepts that shaped
our world / R. C. Sproul.
    p.   cm.
  Includes bibliographical references and index.
  ISBN 1-58134-172-5 (hardcover : alk. paper)
  1. Philosophy—History. 2. Christianity—Philosophy. I. Title.
B72. S68 2000
190—dc21   00-008637
                                              CIP

15	14	13	12	11	10	09	08	07	06	05	04	03	02	01	00
15	14	13	12	11	10	9	8	7	6	5	4	3	2	1	

CONTENTS

ILLUSTRATIONS

INTRODUCTION:
Why Philosophy?

The summer of 1959: This date marked the end of my sophomore year in college and the tail end of the decade of "Happy
Days." The beloved "Ike" still occupied the Oval Office, the
New York Yankees still dominated major-league baseball, and
the turbulent decade of the Sixties was still a year away.

My biggest concern was summer employment. Many friends
who were engineering students had found lucrative summer jobs
that paid well above the minimum wage. My prospects were
bleak: I was a philosophy major. I did not find in the newspaper
a single want ad calling for philosophers. My only real option was
a job for unskilled labor paying the minimum wage. Even at that
I was delighted to be offered work in the maintenance depart-
ment of a hospital.

When the foreman heard I was a philosophy major, he handed
me a broom and said, "Here, you can think all you want while
you're leaning on the broom." My coworkers enjoyed this
calumny. Among other responsibilities, I was to sweep the hospital's driveway and parking area.

During my first week on the job, I was reaching the end of
my sweeping territory. My zone ended where the main hospital
driveway intersected the parking lot of the nurses' home. I noticed
another man sweeping the adjacent parking lot. He greeted me,
and we exchanged names and pleasantries. When I told him I
was a college student, he asked what I was studying. When I said
philosophy, his face brightened and his eyes lit up. He fired a
barrage of questions at me, inquiring about Descartes, Plato,

Hegel, Kant, Kierkegaard, and others. I was astonished at this man's knowledge. He obviously knew far more about philosophy than I did.

"Dangerous" Thoughts

I thought it bizarre that an adult whose chief occupation is to sweep driveways could be so erudite in the abstract field of philosophy. The whole conversation seemed incongruous to me. I had to ask him how he knew so much about philosophy. His story was heart-wrenching.

My new friend was from Germany. He had his Ph.D. in philosophy and had been a professor of philosophy in Berlin. When Adolf Hitler came to power, the Nazis were not content to find a "final solution" for Jews and Gypsies. They also sought to eliminate intellectuals whose ideas were at odds with the "values" of the Third Reich. My friend was removed from his position. When he spoke out against the Nazis, his wife and all but one of his children were arrested and executed. He escaped from Germany with his young daughter.

When I asked why he was no longer teaching, he said that teaching philosophy had destroyed the lives of his loved ones and ruined his own. With tears in his eyes, he said he now lived only for his daughter.

When I heard this man's story, I was twenty years old. To me World War II was a dim memory. To a twenty-year-old, fourteen years seem like an eternity. But to my German friend, who was in his mid-fifties, the war years seemed like yesterday. His memory of the past was by no means dim.

I mused on something else that morning, which is why I am recounting the tale here. I was pushing a broom because I lived in a culture that sees little value in philosophy and gives scant esteem to those who pursue it. My friend was pushing a broom, on the other hand, because he came from a culture that gave great weight to philosophy. His family was destroyed because Hitler understood that ideas are dangerous. Hitler so feared the consequences of my friend's ideas that he did everything possible to eliminate him—and his ideas.

As you read this book, you probably are not outside reading by sunlight or inside reading by candlelight. More likely you are reading in a room illumined by artificial light. Where did that light come from? You probably got to where you are right now by automobile. Where did that car come from? There is probably no outhouse behind your kitchen. Your place of residence probably has running water and indoor plumbing. Where did that come from?

I ask about things that were virtually unknown just a century ago, but that we now consider essential elements of everyday living. These practical things are there because someone first thought about them (perhaps while leaning on a broom) before they were invented or brought into existence. The idea preceded the product, which is how it usually works.

Not all ideas issue in tangible products. Some ideas are harebrained. Yet even a dreamer's fanciful ideas often become honed into sharp concepts with massive consequences.

Foundational Thoughts

Philosophy forces us to think foundationally. By *foundational* I mean first principles or basic truths. Most ideas that shape our lives are accepted (at least initially) somewhat uncritically. We do not create a world or environment from scratch and then live in it. Rather we step into a world and culture that already exists, and we learn to interact with it.

For example, few people today debate the virtues of a graduated or progressive income tax, in which one group pays not only more money but also a higher percentage of their income (how unlike the tithe—God's "flat tax"!). Rarely does anyone challenge the justness of such a scheme, because it has been in force for so long. It is an accepted reality. When enacted, however, it was the focus of fierce controversy.

Nor do we find much deep discussion about political or legal theory, such as marked the Enlightenment. Then, when the structure of monarchy was giving way to new forms of government, people focused on foundational theory. But today (except perhaps during impeachment trials) we rarely hear discussions of the difference between a republic and a democracy. Nor do we hear loud controversies about the foundation for law (save when Supreme Court-justice nominee Clarence Thomas alluded to natural law during his confirmation hearing and Senator Joseph Biden responded with a heated retort).

Our country's Constitution was established more than 200 years ago. This idea has already been implemented. Today we merely tweak it with new legislation here and a new judicial decision there. Never mind that we have tweaked the original beyond recognition and are in danger of being pecked to death by baby ducks.

We step into the game long after the game was conceived. The rules have been decided and the boundaries set. We are amused when Descartes labors so long and thinks so deeply in order to conclude that he exists. We think it is funny; we think it a foolish waste of time to prove something we all know is true— that we exist. Or we are puzzled by Kant's spending his life analyzing *how* we know anything that we know, when from our vantage point we simply know it.

Or do we? Thinkers like Descartes and Kant are not merely gazing at their navels. Foundational thinking lays bare all of our assumptions so that we may discover those assumptions that are false and often lethal. Foundational thinking cares about the difference between truth and falsehood because it cares about good and evil. The ancient maxim still applies: "The unexamined life is not worth living." To any serious thinker, and especially to the professing Christian, an unexamined life is not an option.

If my thinking has no value in the marketplace or is not esteemed in the court of public opinion, I can always go back to sweeping parking lots. But I cannot *not* think. To not think is unthinkable.

This book is written not for philosophy scholars but for laypersons—albeit educated laypersons. I hope it serves as an enticing foretaste for future study of theoretical thought. I have intentionally avoided the apparatus of technicalia, which tends to intimidate the laity. In addition to using primary sources, I have leaned on experts in the history of philosophy: Roger Scruton, Gordon Clark, Samuel Stumpf, and others.[1] I hope you find this overview of the history of ideas helpful.

R. C. Sproul
Orlando
January 2000

1
The
First Philosophers

The origins of Western philosophy are rooted in the ancient Aegean world. A sharp distinction between science and philosophy was unknown to thinkers of that day. The word *science* in its etymology simply means "knowledge," and the term *philosophy* derives from "love of wisdom." As ancient man sought to understand himself and the world around him, knowledge and wisdom were interrelated ideas. He was concerned about the nature of things.

Philosophy was born in the ancient quest for ultimate reality, the reality that transcends the proximate and commonplace and that defines and explains the data of everyday experience. Three burdens dominated the thinking of the original philosophers: first, a quest for "monarchy"; second, a quest for unity in the midst of diversity; and third, a quest for cosmos over chaos. Though these quests may be distinguished at one level, at a different level all three involve the search for a metaphysical answer to the physical world.

What is meant here by *monarchy* may be understood by a brief analysis of the word's original meaning. The term *monarchy* is made up of a prefix and a root. The prefix *mono* means "one, singular." The root, which is more significant, is *archē*, which means "chief, beginning, or root." It is often used as a prefix in English, as in *archbishops, archenemies, archetypes, archheretics,* and *archangels.* Here *arch* means "chief, ruler." An archangel is a chief or ruling angel, as an archbishop is a chief or ruling bishop. The later connotation of *monarch* as a political figure rests on the idea of one chief ruler.

In the ancient quest for monarchy, philosophers sought the chief or ruling substance, or *archē*, of which all things are made or from which they exist. It was a search for the supreme essence or substance of things, a quest for the ultimate "stuff" of the real world.

One of the most vexing problems encountered by the ancient thinker (a problem that remains vexing today) was that of unity and diversity, or of "the one and the many." It was a matter of discovering sense amid vastly different manifestations of reality: How do all things fit together in a meaningful way?

Today we speak, often somewhat glibly, of "the universe." The term *universe* is something of a mongrel, in which the words *unity* and *diversity* (the one and the many) are jammed together to coin a single word. Institutions of higher learning are often called "universities" because there the various elements of the universe are studied.

The so-called "analytical method" of the Enlightenment reflected this ancient quest as it sought the "logic" of the facts— that is, as it sought to deduce laws or universals from the raw data of the particulars. It used the scientific method of learning that combines the tools of induction (observing and collecting data) and deduction (drawing logical inferences and conclusions from the data). The logic was that which gave sense, coherence, or unity to the diversity.

In his famous book *Cosmos,*[1] drawn from the television series of the same name, Carl Sagan begins by affirming that the world is cosmos, not chaos. A cosmos is orderly, chaos is not. Chaos is the archenemy of science. If reality is ultimately chaotic, science itself becomes a manifest impossibility.

Perhaps you have heard of "chaos physics." This name suggests a kind of commitment to chaos, but the opposite is the case. Chaos physics probes elements of *apparent* chaos in order to discover patterns of order that lurk beneath the surface. These physicists study such things as the dynamics of fluid motion, the topography of seacoasts, the structure of snowflakes, and the patterns of wind currents that influence weather. In some respects modern chaos theory recapitulates in a more technical and sophisticated manner the pursuit of cosmos by ancient philosophers.

Thales of Miletus

When asked about the ultimate stuff of which humans are composed, we may answer that boys are made of "frogs and snails and puppy-dog tails," while girls are made of "sugar and spice and everything nice." This children's ditty may amuse, but as a scientific analysis of the real differences between the sexes, it obviously does not suffice.

When we look at Thales' answer to the question of ultimate reality, we may conclude that he too was spinning a childish ditty. Thales argued that all is *water*. Everything that *is* is composed of water, and water serves as the unity, the *archei,* of all things.

Before dismissing Thales to the land of fairy tales and mythology, however, we must afford him the benefit of a second glance. One reason Thales is regarded as the father of Western philosophy is that he distanced himself from traditional mythology and poetry. He sought instead a scientific answer to the nature of things. Nor can Thales be dismissed as a primitive blockhead with no eye or brain for real science. Thales can be regarded as a pre-Renaissance Renaissance man whose diverse achievements are

comparable to those of Leonardo da Vinci and rival those of
Archimedes.

Thales solved engineering problems by diverting the flow of
a river. He devised a system of measuring the heights of Egyptian
pyramids based on the movement of their shadows. He developed techniques of navigating by the stars and created an instrument for measuring distances at sea. But his crowning scientific
achievement was his accurate prediction of a solar eclipse that
occurred on May 28, 585 B.C. So much for puppy-dog tails!

Although the original writings of Thales have been lost, some
of his thought can be reconstructed by way of anecdotes told about
him by other ancient writers, their quotations from his writings,
and their allusions to his ideas. We do not know the full measure
of his argument that water is the ultimate reality. Water has several factors to commend itself as the ultimate reality. First, the three
great mysteries of ancient (and contemporary) science are life,
motion, and being. The third is the issue of metaphysical essence.
Thales noted that all things he observed in this world come in innu-
merable sizes, shapes, and colors, and that they all appear in one of
three possible states: liquid, gas, or solid.

To reduce reality to a single element, Thales looked for one
that manifests itself in all three states. The obvious choice is water,
which appears as liquid, steam, or ice. From here it is a short
speculative step to consider all liquids as particular forms of water,
all gases as particular forms of steam, and all solids as particular
forms of ice.

What about the mystery of life? Thales could easily see that
living things are dependent on water. He knew he could not live
long without it. And if he wanted to grow grass from seed, he
knew he had to water the seed. Ancient people linked their survival to the presence of rain and the absence of drought.

Finally, Thales faced the problem of motion: How does one

explain the origin of motion in light of our understanding of the law of inertia—that bodies at rest tend to remain at rest unless acted on by an outside force? The obvious question is, What set that outside force in motion? (The quest for an "unmoved mover" did not begin with Aristotle.)

To solve this part of the puzzle, Thales needed an automobile. No, I do not mean a Buick. Thales sought something that was hylozoistic, something that has the capacity for self-motion (auto-mobile). He needed something that can move itself without being acted on by something else. As he observed the flow of rivers and the constant motion of the tides, water again became an enticing candidate. Before dismissing Thales as being "all wet" for not perceiving the forces of gravity, especially as exercised by the moon on the ebb and flow of tides, we owe him the benefit of the doubt.

Thales was the first philosopher, but by no means the last. He was succeeded by others who sought to correct or refine his theories. The pre-Socratic philosophers can be organized into four distinct camps, depending on their view of the nature of ultimate reality: 1) corporeal monism, 2) incorporeal monism, 3) corporeal pluralism, and 4) incorporeal pluralism. These four categories can

Table 1.1
Ultimate Reality

	Monism	Pluralism
Corporeal	*1. Corporeal monism:* Ultimate reality is physical and one. (Thales)	*3. Corporeal pluralism:* Ultimate reality is physical and more than one. (Empedocles, Anaxagoras)
Incorporeal	*2. Incorporeal monism:* Ultimate reality is nonphysical and one.	*4. Incorporeal pluralism:* Ultimate reality is nonphysical and more than one.

be reduced to two crucial issues: 1) Is ultimate reality physical (corporeal) or nonphysical (incorporeal)? 2) Is ultimate reality one (monism) or more than one (pluralism)?

Thales, seeing water as the one ultimate essence, was a corporeal monist. He was succeeded by his student Anaximander, who rejected the theory that reality can be reduced to one specific element. Anaximander looked for something even more basic, something that rises above or transcends the arena of this world, a world with chronological and spatial boundaries. He searched for a boundless, ultimate realm from which all things come. It is the realm of what he called the *apeiron* or the indeterminate boundless, what we might call the infinite.

Anaximander had a young associate named Anaximenes, who was the last of the group known as the Milesian philosophers. Dissatisfied with the vague idea of a mysterious "boundless," Anaximenes sought to bring philosophy back to earth by combining or synthesizing some of Thales' concerns with those of Anaximander. Anaximenes looked for something that is both specific and spread everywhere. This he found in *air*. Air has many of the same advantages as water: it has different states of rarefaction and condensation, is essential to life, and appears to have the power of self-motion when the wind blows.

Pythagoras

One of the most fascinating groups that preceded Socrates and Plato was the Pythagoreans, people who clearly influenced Plato.

Every high-school student who has taken geometry has heard of the Pythagorean theorem. Pythagoras migrated from Samos to southern Italy, where he developed his theory of numbers. He had a spiritual and religious interest in mathematics by which mystical significance was assigned to numbers. He considered the number ten to be the perfect number. In the study of math, the formal (pertaining to form or essence) becomes more important than the material, the intellectual or spiritual more important than the physical. For Pythagoras and his followers, mathematics is a matter of the soul.

Pythagoreans held music in high regard because of its therapeutic value to the soul. To them music is what "soothes the savage beast." They developed a mathematics of harmony, seeing that sounds can be broken down into numerical ratios or mathematical proportions. Our modern scales owe their origin chiefly to the insight of the Pythagoreans.

Medicine, for Pythagoreans, was also subject to mathematics. They saw bodily health in terms of balance or harmony between such opposites as hot and cold and among the body's chemical functions, anticipating the current biomedical concern for hormonal balances.

Pythagoreans applied mathematics to astronomy, seeking the "harmony of the spheres" in an effort to plot and predict the motion of heavenly bodies. This was no mere exercise in speculation; ancient people depended on the stars not only for navigation but, even more importantly, for measuring time (calendars) so they could plant and harvest their crops at optimum times.

That math has served as a crucial handmaiden to advances in natural science is documented by history. Advances in mathematical theory have ushered in several revolutions such as the Copernican revolution, the revolution initiated by Isaac Newton with his physics, and the revolution in our day of nuclear science.

Two philosophical giants in the pre-Socratic era were Heraclitus and Parmenides. Some have said that all philosophy is nothing more than footnotes to the thought of Plato and Aristotle; one could also argue that Plato and Aristotle were but footnotes to the thought of Heraclitus and Parmenides.

Heraclitus

Heraclitus is sometimes called the "father of modern existentialism" because of his attack on essences. His thought is summarized with the Greek phrase *Panta rhei,* "All things are flowing." According to Heraclitus everything is always and everywhere in flux. To introduce an important philosophical concept here, this means that all things are in a state of *becoming* as distinguished from *being*.

For Heraclitus, whatever *is* is always changing. He illustrated this by declaring that you "cannot step into the same river twice." If you put one foot into a river, by the time you can put your other foot in the river has flowed on. It has changed. Its banks, due to imperceptible erosion, have changed, and you yourself have changed—if in no other way than that you are a few seconds older.

Nevertheless, whatever is changing is still a *something*. Reality is not pure diversity; there remains an abiding unity. Heraclitus looked to fire as the basic element in things because it is constantly in flux. Fire must be constantly fed, yet it constantly gives off something—smoke, heat, or ashes. It is always "in process," always being transformed.

For Heraclitus the process of change is not chaotic but is orchestrated by "God." I put *God* in quotes because for Heraclitus "God" is not a personal being but more like an impersonal force. Flux is the product of a universal reason Heraclitus calls the *logos*. Here we see the philosophical roots of the *logos* concept that the apostle John appropriated to define the preexistent and eternal person of the Godhead who became incarnate. It would be a serious mistake, however, simply to equate or identify John's use of *logos* with that of Greek philosophy, because John filled the term with Hebrew categories of thought. At the same time it would be an equally serious mistake to separate completely John's use of the term from Greek thought.

Heraclitus was looking for a principle of *telos,* a teleology or purpose that would give order and harmony to things in flux, that would give unity to diversity. For him the *logos* is the universal law that is immanent in all things. In the final analysis it is *Fire* with a capital *F.* His system is at root a kind of pantheism.

In examining the presence of flux in all things, Heraclitus sought to account for the reality of strife, which he located in the conflict of opposites. Just as fire works through the conflict of opposites, where nothing is ever lost but only changes its form, so all conflict ultimately is resolved in the overarching fire or the *logos* of things.

Parmenides

Parmenides, a younger contemporary of Heraclitus, founded the Eleatic school of philosophy (so-named for Elea, Italy, where he lived). I first heard of Parmenides while in college. My philosophy professor quoted Parmenides' best-known assertion, "Whatever is, is." I laughed and blurted out, "And he's famous?" With this verbal ejaculation I revealed myself as the quintessential sophomore. I assumed that Parmenides had done nothing more than stutter.

As I reach my twilight years, perhaps the last three holes of the back nine, I have lost the omniscience I briefly enjoyed as a college sophomore. On reflection I can think of no concept I learned in philosophy that has provoked more thought than Parmenides' "Whatever is, is." It forces me to contemplate being itself, which has the salutary benefit of stretching my mind to consider the things of God himself. What I once ridiculed now absorbs me and carries me to the brink of holy apprehension, where I tremble at my own inadequacy.

For Parmenides, if anything exists in an absolute way, it cannot change ("Whatever is, is."). It cannot *be* and *not be* at the same time and in the same way. If it is becoming, it cannot be being. If it is not being, it is nothing. It must *be* absolutely or not at all.

This raises the ultimate philosophical question: Why is there something rather than nothing? If indeed there is something, then there must be being, for without being nothing could be. At the same time, Parmenides understood the principle *Ex nihilo, nihil fit,* "Out of nothing, nothing comes." The idea that something could come out of nothing or that nothing could give rise to something Parmenides rightly considered to be absurd. Manifestly, if ever there were a time when there was nothing, then there would be nothing now.

Change is for Parmenides an illusion. The very concept of change is unthinkable; that is, we cannot really think of it. We cannot think of change because there is no "it" to think about. If something is changing, then in reality it is not an "it." To think of change would require us to think of something in terms of what it is not, which is impossible.

For Parmenides, not only can something not come out of nothing, but also, something cannot arise out of being. If something arises out of being, it already is. Here we see the folly of any concept of self-creation, which requires something to be before it was and which therefore defies all logic. The law of non-contradiction declares that something cannot be what it is and not be what it is at the same time and in the same sense. $A \neq A$

It is important to note, however, that Parmenides was apparently attacking not only the absurd notion of self-creation but also any notion of creation, which by implication includes the Christian notion of creation. Though the Christian notion does not suffer from the absurdities of self-creation, it is nevertheless not without difficulties. The "how" of creation and the way in which the creature's being differs from the creator's remain impenetrable mysteries. (We take comfort, however, that *mystery* is not a synonym of *contradiction*.)

The impasse on the matter of change became a dominant question for later thinkers, who sought to resolve the difficulties between being and becoming. The impasse also provoked a period of skepticism, during which some concluded that the philosophical quest for ultimate reality is a fool's errand, doomed to failure.

Zeno of Elea

Zeno of Elea was a student of Parmenides who devoted himself to answering his mentor's critics. The "common sense" critics argued that the five senses confirm the outward reality of physical things that are many and that undergo change. Sense perception proves the reality of physical things.

Zeno set out to prove that the senses deal only with *appearances* and not with *reality*. To prove that the senses can easily deceive us, Zeno set forth four arguments or paradoxes. To answer the pluralists, who declared that the world is divisible, with discrete units, Zeno used the illustration of a racetrack: To circle the track, the runner must traverse an infinite number of points in a finite number of moments. The runner would first need to reach the halfway point. Then he would need to go halfway to the end from there, then another halfway, and another, all the way to infinity, never reaching the finish line.

The second paradox concerns a race between Achilles and a

tortoise: To give the slow tortoise a chance, Achilles gives him a head start. To beat the tortoise Achilles must first catch up to the tortoise. In the time that it takes Achilles to reach the spot where the tortoise began the race (with his head start), the tortoise has moved on. This process continues forever so that Achilles is always chasing the tortoise but never catching him.

The third paradox involves an archer and an arrow: An arrow in flight must always occupy a space equal to its length. But for an arrow to occupy a space equal to its length, at that moment it must be at rest. Since the arrow always occupies a space equal to its length, it must always be at rest. Hence the arrow's "motion" is an illusion.

The fourth paradox, like the others, demonstrates the relativity of motion in terms similar to those used today, which indicates that motion has no clear definition.

Empedocles

Zeno's skepticism concerning matter and motion was challenged by the Sicilian philosopher Empedocles. He argued that the reality of motion (and change, which is a form of motion) is too obvious to deny. He located the problem in Parmenides' monism and countered with a philosophy of pluralism. His pluralism was corporeal, with reality being composed of immutable and eternal particles. These particles possess "being" and do not change. The objects composed of these particles, however, do change, as they undergo changes in their composition. Empedocles identified four basic elements: earth, air, fire, and water. (This led later thinkers to look for a transcendent element, a "fifth essence," that would unite the four, thus creating the word *quintessence*.) For Empedocles, motion and change were explained by equal and opposite forces in nature that attract and repel each other. He called these forces love and hate, or harmony and discord. The governing principle of harmony is love, which "makes the world go round."

Anaxagoras

Anaxagoras made a major contribution to the pre-Socratic era with a single modification of corporeal pluralism. He viewed the material world as being composed of eternal units called "seeds" or *spermata*. Unique to Anaxagoras was his view that reality is composed not only of matter but also of mind. In searching for a rational principle to bring order and harmony to the seeds of a material world, he developed his concept of the *nous*. The Greek term *nous* means "mind," and from it we get the English adjective *noetic*, "pertaining to the mind." Still, Anaxagoras did not fill his con-

Table 1.2
The First Philosophers

	Century (B.C.)	Birth–death (approx.)	Place of birth	Primary place of residence	Major work
Thales	6th			Miletus, Asia Minor	
Pythagoras	6th	570–497	Samos	Croton, Italy	
Heraclitus	6th–5th	540–480		Ephesus, Asia Minor	*On Nature*
Parmenides	5th			Elea, Italy	*The Way of Truth and the Way of Seeming*
Zeno	5th			Elea, Italy	Title unknown
Empedocles	5th	495–435	Acragas, Sicily	Acragas, Sicily	*On Nature, Purifications*
Anaxagoras	5th	500–428	Clazomenae, Asia Minor	Athens	Title unknown

cept of *nous* with the idea of a personal creator or governor of the universe. His concept was more abstract, an impersonal power or force that is the teleological (purposeful) principle of reality.

Other developments in pre-Socratic philosophy include the primitive atomism of Democritus and the rise of ancient skepticism. We will examine the impact of skepticism on Plato's great mentor, Socrates, in the following chapter.

2

Plato:
Realist and Idealist

One cannot grasp the historical significance of Plato without first considering the impact of his mentor, Socrates. Since Socrates left no body of literature and since he frequently stars as the supreme sage in Plato's *Dialogues*,[1] it is difficult to discern where Socrates leaves off and Plato begins.

Socrates, the "gadfly of Athens," was born in 470 B.C. He grew up during the golden age of Greek culture, a period that witnessed the genius of Euripides and Sophocles in literature, the influence of Pericles in politics, and the building of the Parthenon. The war with Persia was over, and victorious Athens had emerged as a major naval power.

Athens's gilded age, however, was short-lived. Her gold began to tarnish under the burden of the heavy taxation levied by Pericles. This sparked the Peloponnesian War in 431, which ended in 404 with the defeat of Athens. Meanwhile a crass politicization of education, economics, law, and public works led to a decline in both substantive thinking and civic virtue, both of which are enemies to any democratic enterprise that thrives on compromise and the relativization of ethics. Cynicism and skepticism sapped Greek culture of its grandeur. The ancient quest for the *archē* or ultimate reality had given way to a new kind of skepticism and pragmatism. This new mood was incarnated by the Sophists of the fifth century B.C.

Sophism

From the Sophists of antiquity are derived the terms *sophistry,*
sophomoric, and the pejorative use of *sophisticated.* The three
most famous leaders of this movement were Gorgias, Protagoras,
and Thrasymachus.

Gorgias is known for introducing radical skepticism. He
turned his back on philosophy and practiced rhetoric instead. This
discipline focused on the art of persuasion in public discourse. The
goal of rhetoric was not to proclaim truth but to achieve practical aims by persuasion. Rhetoric in this sense functioned in antiquity as Madison Avenue does today.

Gorgias denies that there is any truth. "All statements," he
declares, "are false." It doesn't seem to bother him that if all
statements are false, then the statement "All statements are
false" is also false, meaning that at least some statements must
be true. His views are not unlike those of modern relativists who
proclaim that there are no absolutes (except for the absolute that
there are no absolutes!). He bases his axiom on the premise
that nothing exists. He hedges his bet, however, by saying that
if something does exist, it is unknowable or incomprehensible.
Even if it does exist and is knowable, he argues, it remains
incommunicable.

The views of Gorgias and others served to arouse Socrates
from his dogmatic slumber, as the skepticism of David Hume
would awaken Immanuel Kant centuries later. Socrates realized
that the death of truth would mean the death of virtue, and that
the death of virtue would spell the death of civilization. Without
truth and virtue the only possible outcome is barbarianism.

Thrasymachus, who appears as a foil for Plato in *The
Republic,*[2] is a Sophist who attacks the quest for justice. According
to Thrasymachus, far from being an immoral person, the unjust

person, realizing that crime does pay, is a superior person with superior intellect. Here Thrasymachus anticipates Friedrich Nietzsche's *Übermensch* ("superman"). Justice, says Thrasymachus, is a concept for the weak-minded person who lacks the will to assert himself. Those who rise to the level of true masters are those who prefer injustice. Here is the philosophy of "might is right" with a vengeance, the philosophy of barbarianism. Anticipating Karl Marx, Thrasymachus sees law as nothing more than a reflection of the ruling class's vested interests.

Protagoras, probably the most influential Sophist in Athens, is frequently described by modern historians as the "father of ancient humanism." His famous maxim, *"Homo mensura,"* declares that "man is the measure of all things," of the existence of things that are and of the nonexistence of things that are not.

From a biblical perspective, of course, the honor of being the first humanist does not belong to Protagoras. Indeed, it is accorded not to a man, but to a serpent whose maxim was *"Sicut erat Dei,"* "You will be like God" (Gen. 3:4).

For Protagoras, knowledge begins and ends with man. All human knowledge is limited to our perceptions, and perceptions differ from person to person. Objective truth is neither possible nor desirable. Ultimately (if there is an ultimate) there is no discernible difference between appearance and reality. Perception is reality. Thus something can be true for one person and false for another.

This is true, of course, with respect to preferences. I may prefer chocolate ice cream and you may prefer vanilla. But Protagoras goes beyond the subjective aspect of preference to reduce all reality to preference. This makes scientific knowledge manifestly impossible, as no standards or norms exist to distinguish truth from error. If you prefer to believe that two plus two equals five, then for you it does.

Table 2.1
Sophists

	Century (B.C.)	Birth–death (approx.)	Place of birth	Primary place of residence	Major work
Gorgias	5th		Leontini, Sicily	Athens	*On Not-Being*
Thrasy-machus	5th		Greece		See Plato's *Republic*, bk 1
Protagoras	5th	490–420	Abdera		See Plato's *Protagoras*

Protagoras argues that ethics are likewise merely a matter of preference. Moral rules merely express customs or conventions, which are never really right or wrong. The distinction between vice and virtue rests on the preferences of a given society. The Roman Seneca would say that when vice becomes a society's custom or accepted convention, it is almost impossible to remove.

Protagoras takes the same approach with respect to metaphysics and theology. Though he acknowledges that some people "prefer" religion and that this is fine for them, he says: "About the gods, I am not able to know whether they exist or do not exist, nor what they are like in form; for the factors preventing knowledge are many: the obscurity of the subject and the shortness of human life."

Socrates

Into this milieu of Sophism stepped Socrates. Socrates was no more ready to abandon the quest for truth than to stand back and watch civilization crumble. Some have argued that in his era Socrates was the savior of Western civilization. He realized that knowledge and virtue are inseparable—so much so that virtue

could be defined as right knowledge. Right thinking and right doing can be distinguished from each other, but they can never be separated.

The method of discovering truth attributed to Socrates is that of the dialogue. In the early dialogues of Plato, Socrates is the protagonist. Scholars debate whether the person depicted in these dialogues is the real, historical Socrates or merely a beloved character through whom Plato expresses his own ideas. In either case there remains little doubt that Socrates did invent the so-called "Socratic method."

The Socratic method of discerning truth is to ask provocative questions. Assumptions are challenged as each question probes deeper into the matter at hand. Socrates was convinced that to gain knowledge one must first admit one's ignorance. This admission is the beginning of knowledge, but by no means the goal or end of knowledge. It is a necessary condition for learning. For Socrates, however, unlike the skeptics, knowledge is possible through learning.

Socrates was persistent in his quest for accurate definitions, which are essential to true learning and precise communication. For example, he believed that there is such a thing as justice, though justice may be difficult to define precisely. Anticipating the Enlightenment, Socrates used an analytical method by which he sought the logic of the facts. For him the logic is what is left after the facts are exhausted. "Beauty remains," he said, "after the rose fades." He sought the universals that are gleaned from an examination of the particulars.

Socrates was a martyr to the cause of philosophy. His endless questioning of Athenians, focusing on issues of morality and customs, made them suspicious of him. This was particularly true of his challenging the behavior of young men from the patrician class. One of Socrates' students, a man named Alcibiades, betrayed Athenian secrets to the Spartans. As a result, Socrates was viewed as a mentor to traitors and was brought to trial. He was accused of not worshiping the gods of the state, of introducing strange religious practices, and of corrupting the city's youth. The prosecutor demanded the death penalty. Socrates eschewed compromise as a means of escape and chose instead to drink the hemlock, the means of execution. His dramatic death is chronicled by Plato in the *Phaedo* dialogue.[3]

Plato: Student of Socrates

Plato was born in Athens in 428 B.C. and died at the age of eighty. One tradition is that his name means "broad shoulders," a nickname he received in his youth when he exhibited prowess as a wrestler. Before meeting Socrates, Plato was interested in poetry, an interest that continued and is evident in his later literary style. He studied with Socrates while in his twenties. After his mentor's death, Plato left Athens and traveled abroad, where he encountered the Pythagoreans. While in Sicily, according to one legend, he was kidnapped, put on sale at a slave-market, ransomed by a friend, and sent back to Athens. At age forty he founded the Academy, for which he is famous.

A member of the Athenian aristocracy, Plato's father was a descendant of the early kings of Athens. The Academy was so named because Plato received a tract of land outside of Athens from a benefactor named Academia. The Academy, situated in a grove of olive trees, is the source of the expression "the groves of Academe."

A sign posted above the entrance to the Academy read, "Let none but geometers enter here." To the modern observer this sign implies that the school taught only mathematics. Plato's real passion, however, was philosophy. The link to geometry is this:

Both math and philosophy may be considered *formal* sciences (pertaining to form or essence), as distinguished from the physical or *material* sciences. Plato maintained a keen interest in mathematics and its concern with abstract forms, an issue that was central to his thought.

At the heart of Plato's elaborate philosophical theory was his desire to "save the phenomena." "Phenomena" refers to those things that are evident or manifest to our senses. The task of science, in simple terms, is to explain reality. Scientific paradigms shift as they seek more accurate and comprehensive explanations for observed reality. Thus, to "save the phenomena" is to construct a theory that explains reality with a minimum of anomalies. An anomaly is a datum that does not fit the pattern or cannot be explained by a current model or paradigm; the paradigm is forced to shift when the anomalies become too severe or numerous. Plato's passion for "saving the phenomena" helped to build the philosophical foundation for science.

Plato's paradigm was designed to resolve the tension between Parmenides and Heraclitus, the tension between flux and permanence, becoming and being. Using the later Hegelian terms of a dialectic, we could say that the thought of Heraclitus (becoming and flux) was a thesis and the thought of Parmenides (being and permanency) was its antithesis; Plato then sought a synthesis that would account for both change and permanence, that would incorporate both being and becoming as poles of a dialectic that seems to be demanded by a comprehensive view of reality.

Theory of Ideas

It is sometimes confusing for students to hear Plato described as both a realist and an idealist. In modern nomenclature the terms are used as antonyms. An idealist tends to view the world through

Figure 2.1
Plato's Synthesis

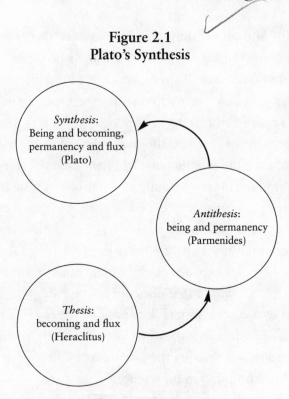

rose-colored glasses and ignores the harsh side of reality. Conversely a realist has a jaundiced eye toward lofty ideals and focuses instead on the warts and blemishes of life.

When the terms *idealist* and *realist* are both applied to Plato, something different is in view. He was an idealist because of the central significance he attached to *Ideas* (with a capital *I*). He was a realist because he argued that ideas are not merely mental constructs or *names (nomina)* but real entities.

Plato conceived of two different "worlds." The primary world or sphere of reality is the world of ideas. This metaphysical realm lies beyond or behind the realm of material things. For Plato the world of ideas is not only real but also "more real" than the world of physical objects.

For Plato the realm of ideas is the realm of true knowledge.

The realm of material objects is the realm of mere opinion. His famous analogy of the cave illustrates this. In *The Republic* Plato tells an imaginary story of men who have lived in a cave as prisoners since childhood. They are chained and immobile. Their field of vision is restricted to a wall directly in front of them. Behind them is an elevated area where people are walking, carrying objects made of wood, stone, and other materials. The glow from a fire casts shadows of the people on the wall that the prisoners can see. The prisoners hear the voices of those people and assume that the voices come from the shadows. Indeed, their only perception of reality comes from the shadows.

Plato then asks what would happen if one of the prisoners were to be released and allowed to walk toward the fire. Having been cramped for so many years, he would find walking painful. The glowing fire would hurt his eyes. Because looking at real objects is more painful than gazing at shadows, he would be inclined to return to his customary position and confine his glance to the familiar shadows.

Suppose the prisoner were dragged out of the cave and into the midday sun. The pain in his eyes would be intensified. Soon, however, his eyes would grow accustomed to the light and he could see things clearly. This would be a grand epiphany for him. If, however, he were then forced to return to the cave and tried to explain his new understanding of reality, he would be ridiculed. "If they could lay hands on the man who was trying to set them free and lead them up," said Plato, "they would kill him," perhaps an allusion to the fate of his beloved mentor, Socrates.

For Plato, knowledge that is restricted to the material world is at best mere opinion and at worst ignorance. The task of education is to lead people out of darkness into light, out of the cave and its shadows and into the noonday sun. The Latin term *educare* describes this process. Its root meaning is "to lead out of,"

as the root *ducere* means "to lead." We remember the title of
Benito Mussolini, *"Il Duce,"* meaning "the leader."

Plato saw people living in two different worlds: the world of
ideas and the world of physical objects. He called material objects
"receptacles"—things that receive or contain something else. The
physical object contains its idea or form. The form is distinguished
from the object. The form causes the essence of a thing. In this
sense a material object participates in or imitates its ideal form.
But it is at best a copy of the ideal form, and an imperfect copy
at that.

This concept of the relationship between form and matter,
idea and receptacle, lies at the heart of the Greek view of the inherent imperfection of all things material, which led inevitably to
the denigration of physical things. This negative view of physical
reality influenced many Christian theologies.

Theory of Recollection

Plato's ontology (his theory of the nature of being) had a major
impact on his epistemology (his theory of the nature of knowing). The theory of recollection is frequently called the theory of
reminiscence. Both recollection and reminiscence involve an act of
remembering or recalling.

To understand this view, let us ask the following question:
When you think about a chair, what idea or concept comes to your
mind? A wooden, ladder-back chair? A folding metal chair? An
overstuffed lounge chair? Or perhaps a rocking chair? These are
but a few examples of a vast variety of objects we call "chairs."

How would we define the common characteristics or the
"essence" of a chair? Would we say simply that a chair is "an
object you sit on"? This would be inadequate. We sit on objects
that we do not call chairs. There is a difference between a chair

and a sofa, a chair and a bench, a chair and a stool. We could say a chair has four legs, but some have fewer, some have more, and rocking chairs have none at all.

Even Plato found it difficult at times to define things accurately. When seeking a precise definition for *man*, he settled for a while on the definition "a featherless biped." Then one of his students, hiding behind a wall, threw over it a plucked chicken with a sign attached that read, "Plato's man."

Plato argued that in the ideal world a perfect idea of chair or "chairness" exists. Our soul comes from the ideal world already possessing the knowledge of the ideal chair. That knowledge is obscured but not obliterated by the body, the soul's prison. The body is the cave in which the soul or mind is held captive. Chairs that we perceive in the physical world are shadows or imperfect copies of the real, ideal chair. We recognize chairs as chairs insofar as they approximate the perfect idea of chairness that is innate in our minds.

We are reminded of the Supreme Court's attempt to define pornography. "I may not be able to define pornography," said one justice, "but I know it when I see it." Likewise, we may be unable to define a chair precisely or exhaustively, but we know one when we see it. Plato would explain this by saying that our encounter with a physical chair, which is a receptacle or imperfect copy of the ideal chair or the idea of chairness, stimulates our memory of the perfect idea of chair. Therefore we call it a chair.

Plato developed this theme in several dialogues. In *Meno*,[4] Socrates leads an uneducated young slave into articulating the Pythagorean theorem. By asking the lad the right questions, Socrates gets him to recollect the formal truth from the deepest recesses of his soul or mind.

For Plato, knowledge comes, not from experience *(a posteriori),* but through reason *(a priori).* Ultimate ideas are innate and not discovered from experience. The best the senses can do is to awaken the consciousness to what it already knows. At worst the senses can mislead the mind. Teaching is a form of midwifery, in which the teacher only assists the student in giving birth to an idea that is already there.

Plato put a premium on the mind. No wonder he put up the sign, "Let none but geometers enter here." The mind or soul is tripartite, according to Plato—composed of reason, spirit, and appetite. Reason includes the awareness of a value or goal. The spirit is the drive toward action under reason's impulse. Appetite is the desire for physical things. We experience moral conflict when the spirit is opposed by the appetite. They are like horses pulling us in opposite directions. The good or virtuous life is dominated by contemplative reason.

The true philosopher cannot be satisfied with empirical or sensory knowledge, which is not ideal knowledge but the shadowy knowledge of opinion—the "knowledge" of the cave. The true philosopher reaches for the essence of things, for the ideals. This allows the philosopher to rise above the superficiality of Sophism and the skepticism of the materialists. He seeks the universal and is dissatisfied with a list of particulars. After discerning that a particular object is beautiful or virtuous, he moves beyond that particular to discover the very essence of beauty and virtue. Something is good only insofar as it participates in or imitates the perfect idea of the good, and this ideal was Plato's god.

Since Plato, philosophy has never stopped wrestling with the metaphysical status of ideas, the relationship between the formal and the material, and the relationship between the mind and the senses.

3

Aristotle:
The Philosopher

It is no accident that, when students of philosophy refer to "the philosopher," everyone in the group recognizes the allusion to Aristotle. Aristotle earned the title "the philosopher" by the prodigious scope and depth of his work. He taught a wide variety of subjects, including logic, rhetoric, poetry, ethics, biology, physics, astronomy, political theory, economics, aesthetics, and anatomy—not to mention metaphysical philosophy.

Aristotle was born in 384 B.C. in Thrace. His father was the personal physician of the king of Macedonia. At age seventeen Aristotle went to Athens. He enrolled in Plato's Academy and studied there for twenty years. Aristotle distinguished himself under Plato's tutelage but presumably provoked jealousy and animosity in other students. Despite being the Academy's most celebrated alumnus, he was twice passed over for the position of Plato's successor, possibly making him the first victim of academic politics.

Around 347 B.C. Aristotle left Athens and went to Assos, near Troy. He spent three years in the king's court, where he married the king's adopted daughter. When Aristotle and his wife returned to Athens, she died. He then entered into a union with a woman named Herphylis, who bore him a son, Nicomachus (for whom the *Nicomachean Ethics*[1] is named).

In 342 Aristotle was summoned to Macedonia by King Philip

II and appointed personal tutor of the king's son, Alexander. This relationship would have a massive impact not only on the Mediterranean world in the immediate future but also on Western civilization throughout history. Aristotle's star pupil would distinguish himself not as a philosopher but as a military leader. Alexander the Great gained from his mentor a passion for unity. His military conquests were motivated in large measure by his desire to create a unified culture in the ancient world, a culture united by a common language, Greek. Because this program of Hellenization extended to Palestine, the New Testament was written in Greek rather than in Hebrew or Latin.

Alexander was also interested in the acquisition of knowledge. Some have argued that the best-funded government-sponsored scientific expedition prior to the modern American space program was the one connected with Alexander's military expeditions. A virtual army of scientists marched with his soldiers for the express purpose of collecting flora and fauna and of classifying and analyzing these specimens.

In 334 B.C. Aristotle returned to Athens and founded his own school, the Lyceum. The campus boasted a tree-covered walkway, the Peripatos. Aristotle would stroll along this walkway and lecture to his students following behind him. This earned for the Lyceum the title "the peripatetic school." This method of teaching while walking was later imitated by others, the most famous being Jesus of Nazareth, whose disciples (or pupils) literally "followed" him.

Aristotle presided over the Lyceum for thirteen years, involved in scientific studies and in writing—his literary output was massive. After Alexander the Great died in 323 B.C., a fierce anti-Macedonian sentiment arose, which caught Aristotle in its wake because of his connection to Alexander. Like Socrates earlier, Aristotle was charged with impiety. He fled to Chaleis, where about a year later he died of natural causes.

Logic

When we hear Aristotle's name we often think first of "Aristotelian logic." Other refined and modified systems of logic have been developed since Aristotle's day, but he laid the foundation of formal logic.

Aristotle did not invent logic any more than Columbus "invented" America. What Aristotle did was to define logic and set forth its fundamentals. In one sense he did not view logic as a separate science with its own field of inquiry, such as botany, physics, chemistry, and many other disciplines; rather, he saw logic as the *organon* or instrument of all science.

As an organon, logic is the supreme tool necessary for all other sciences. It is the necessary condition for science even to be possible. This is because logic is essential to intelligible discourse. That which is illogical is unintelligible; it is not only not understood, but is also incapable of being understood. That which is illogical represents chaos, not cosmos. And absolute chaos cannot be known in an orderly way, making knowledge or *scientia* a manifest impossibility.

Logic itself has no material content and in this regard may be seen as a *formal* science, much like mathematics, which in some respects is a form of symbolic logic. Logic measures or analyzes the relationships of statements or propositions. It can show that the conclusion of a syllogism is valid or invalid; it does not determine the truth of a conclusion or argument. Arguments are not true or false, but valid or invalid. *Statements* may be either true or false, but the logical relationship of one statement to another is either valid or invalid.

Aristotle wrote about the fundamental laws of logic, including the law of "noncontradiction." The chief principle of logic is the law of noncontradiction: Something cannot *be* what it is and *not be* what it is at the same time and in the same sense or relationship. *A* cannot be *A* and *-A* (non-*A*) at the same time and in the same relationship. We may be able to predicate (affirm or deny) many things about the same subject, but we cannot predicate of a subject its negative. For example, we can say that a man is tall, short, rich, poor, old, young, a brother, a son, or a father, but we cannot say that the man is not a man. Likewise, we can say that he is a father and a son at the same time, but we can't say this of him in the same relationship. Contrary to the popular ditty, "I am my own grandpa," I cannot be my own biological grandfather.

It is crucial to understand that in formulating the laws of logic, Aristotle was concerned not only about our thinking about things but also about the existence of the things we think about. Though Aristotle finally rejected Plato's philosophy, he certainly was concerned about the relationship between thought and reality.

Though we call logic a "formal" science, to Aristotle it was by no means merely formal. Aristotle's concern for truth was also a concern for reality, for the two are inseparably related. The very word for truth in Greek, *alētheia,* means, among other things, "real state of affairs." According to Aristotle, the laws of logic apply to all sciences because they are valid for all reality.

This is not to say that all that is rational is real. We can conceive of ideas that are logical but do not correspond to reality. For example, the idea or concept of a unicorn is not illogical, but unicorns do not exist in reality. Everything that *is* real, however, is rational. The illogical cannot exist in reality. There cannot be in reality a non-unicorn unicorn. This does not mean that people never violate the law of noncontradiction and thereby indulge in illogical thinking. This happens frequently. But when we begin to think in this manner, at that point we lose touch with reality.

For instance, the idea of an immovable object is perfectly

logical; so is the idea of an irresistible force. What is not logical is the idea of a real immovable object and a real irresistible force coexisting. The two cannot both exist in the real world. Why? What would happen in the real world if an irresistible force met an immovable object? As the songwriter understood, something would have to give. If the irresistible force moves the immovable object, then the immovable object is in fact movable. If it is movable, it cannot at the same time and in the same relationship be immovable. On the other hand, if the immovable object does not move, the irresistible force is in fact resistible. A force cannot be both resistible and irresistible at the same time and in the same relationship.

Again, reality may contain *something* that is itself both immovable and irresistible in its force, but it cannot contain *one* thing that is absolutely immovable and *another* that is absolutely irresistible.

For Aristotle, the law of noncontradiction is not merely a law of thought but also a law of being. Indeed it is a law of thought precisely because it is first a law of being.

People can *say* that the number five is both odd and even, but it cannot be both odd and even, because the terms are mutually exclusive. We may *say* it is both, but we cannot intelligibly *think* it is both.

The Categories

In defining how we think about things, Aristotle developed the concept of *categories*. This concept is vital to an understanding of language and knowledge. Knowledge implies a certain awareness of objects in reality. We assign names to these objects or we use words to describe them. Ideas involve *words*.

Biology, for example, has a subdivision called taxonomy, the science of classification. Biological entities are sorted into king-dom, phylum, class, order, family, genus, and species. We distin-guish between the animal kingdom and the plant kingdom. In the former we further distinguish between mammals and rep-tiles, vertebrates and invertebrates. This process of classification notes two things: similarities and differences. We group ideas according to their similarities and distinguish them according to their differences. We group birds together because they have feath-ers and wings, and fish because they have fins and gills. But not all birds are woodpeckers and not all fish are minnows.

The science of taxonomy is crucial not to biology alone but to all science, because it is crucial to all knowledge. It is crucial to all knowledge because it is crucial to all language. Knowledge depends on language for its intelligibility. All meaningful words reflect the properties of similarity and difference. A word that means everything actually means nothing. To be meaningful a word must both affirm something and deny something. It must refer to what it is and not refer to what it is not. In this sense all science is taxonomy, because taxonomy involves the content of discrete ideas that can be distinguished from the content of other discrete ideas. The more complex and discriminate knowledge becomes, the more precise the science. We are grateful a physi-cian can distinguish between a stomachache caused by indigestion and one caused by stomach cancer, because the treatment for each differs significantly.

When we think about something, we think about subjects and their predicates (those things that can be affirmed or denied about them). This is what Aristotle was getting at with his doctrine of categories. For him the categories refer to ideas that can be pred-icated of a particular substance. These categories include *quantity, quality, relations, place, date, posture, possession, action,* and *pas-sivity.* For example, we may state that a man is six feet tall. The term *man* is the *substance* we are describing. The predicate "six feet tall" tells us something about his *quantity*. If we say he is short or gifted, we are speaking about a *quality* he possesses. If we say he is in Miami, we say something of his *place* or location.

These nine categories, according to Aristotle, refer to all possible predicates about a thing. They are all possible meanings attached to the verb *is*. For Aristotle the tenth (or first) category is substance itself. If I say, "Socrates is a man," I am predicating something about Socrates' substance. Every reality must have a substance or it would be nothing. Its substance is its essential reality. The Sophists argued against the law of noncontradiction and asserted that the same thing can be a man and a mouse, meaning it can be both man and non-man at the same time and in the same relationship. Aristotle said this is absurd. Those who argue against the law of noncontradiction must also deny substantive reality.

According to Aristotle, an entity is made up of its substance and its predicates, or what he called its *accidens*. The primary category of a thing is its substance, its essential nature. Some men may be tall, others short. Some men are fat, others thin. Some men are rich, others poor. But all of them are men. Manhood is the universal essence found in all men. While men may differ with respect to particular qualities or categories, there is a substratum of manness in all of them. This *sub*stance stands "under" or "beneath" all of its qualities.

The language of Aristotle was used in the Christian church to define many theological concepts. One example is the term *transubstantiation,* used by the Roman Catholic Church to define the miracle of the mass. Aristotle had distinguished between the substance and the accidens of a thing. The substance is its essential nature, while its accidens are its external, perceivable qualities. An oak tree has the accidens of tallness and hardness because these accidens are connected to the substance of the tree. The doctrine of transubstantiation maintains that in the mass the substance of bread and wine are miraculously transformed into the substance of the body and blood of Christ, while the accidens of the bread and wine remain the same. This transaction involves a double miracle. On the one hand, you have the substance of the body and blood of Christ present *without* the *accidens* of the body and blood of Christ. On the other hand, you have the accidens of bread and wine *without* the *substance* of bread and wine. This is why the elements still look like bread and wine, taste like bread and wine, and feel like bread and wine.

Though Aristotle's language is used in formulating it, the doctrine of transubstantiation represents a sharp departure from his philosophy. Aristotle allowed for the distinction between an entity's substance and accidens, but not for their separation (as is called for in transubstantiation). He maintained that a thing's accidens are generated by or flow out of its substance. An oak tree has acorns because acorns are part of the accidens of an oak tree's substance. The presence of acorns signals the presence of an oak tree, not the presence of an elephant, because the substance of an elephant does not produce the accidens of acorns. Thus a thing's substance generates its accidens. Of course the Roman Catholic Church understood Aristotle's philosophy at this point and found that a miracle was necessary to transcend the natural connection between substance and accidens.

Form and Matter

Aristotle's theory of form represents his most significant departure from Plato. Aristotle was not satisfied with Plato's synthesis of Heraclitus and Parmenides, of being and becoming. In an attempt to account for both being and becoming, both permanence and change, Plato had postulated two different worlds—one of ideas and one of receptacles. The result was a philosophy that is essentially dualistic. Aristotle's passion for unity led him to break with Plato and construct his own metaphysical theory.

For Aristotle, all substance is a combination of form *and* matter. We never encounter form without matter or matter without form. Forms or ideas have no independent existence apart from matter. There is no ideal realm where forms or ideas exist in and of themselves.

Aristotle is not saying that form or idea is not real. Universals are not mere categories supplied by the mind, or subjective notions or names *(nomina)*. The forms are real, and they exist in individual entities themselves. The form of manness really exists in each individual man. The form of elephantness exists in each individual elephant.

Aristotle explains that the form of a thing—what he calls its "entelechy"—determines its particular materiality. Humans display the attributes of humanity because they contain the form, the entelechy, of humanness. Entelechy is a teleological force or principle that governs a thing's becoming what it becomes. Acorns do not grow into elephants because they contain the entelechy of oak treeness, not elephantness.

The realm of becoming is the realm of change. All change represents a kind of motion. That which changes moves from one thing to another. This does not necessitate a change in location. For example, the process of generation and decay are types of change or motion. Likewise the process of aging is a kind of change or motion. For something to change from one place to another or from one state to another, something must cause that change to take place. The process of becoming requires causation.

The Four Causes

Aristotle posited four distinct types of causes that produce changes in things. These causes are 1) the formal cause, which determines what a thing is; 2) the material cause, that *out of which* a thing is made; 3) the efficient cause, that *by which* a thing is made; and 4) the final cause, that *for which* a thing is made, or its purpose.

Table 3.1
The Four Causes

	Defined	Illustrated
Formal cause	That which determines what a thing is	The sculptor's idea or plan for a sculpture
Material cause	That *out of* which a thing is made	The block of marble
Efficient cause	That *by* which a thing is made	The sculptor
Final cause	That *for* which a thing is made; its purpose	The decoration of a house or garden

For example, what causes a statue to be made? Its formal cause is the artist's idea or plan for it. Its material cause is the block of marble out of which it is carved. Its efficient cause is the sculptor who shapes the marble into the statue. And its final cause is, in all likelihood, to decorate someone's house or garden.

Change does not occur by combining formless matter with matterless form. Rather, changes are always wrought in things that already have a combination of form and matter, that are changed into something new or different. The painter does not create a masterpiece *ex nihilo*. Instead he arranges pigment on a canvas that already exists and arranges the paint in a way that creates a picture.

The dynamic of change, for Aristotle, is bound up with the

ideas of *potentiality* and *actuality*. An oak tree begins with an acorn. The acorn is not actually an oak tree, but it has the potential of becoming one. That potential is realized when it actually becomes an oak tree. But nothing contains any potentiality unless it first has actuality. Actuality is primary, and it is a necessary condition for potentiality. There can be no such thing as pure or absolute potentiality. Such a "thing" would be potentially anything or potentially everything, but it would be actually nothing.

According to Aristotle, however, there can, indeed must, be something that is pure or absolute actuality. This is Aristotle's "god," or his notion of pure being. A being of pure and absolute actuality has no unrealized potential. It is not open to change, growth, or mutation. A being with no potentiality and with pure actuality, since it has no change, must have no motion of any kind. This concept formed Aristotle's idea of the "unmoved mover."

The Unmoved Mover

The ultimate cause of motion, according to Aristotle, must be rooted in pure being or pure actuality. It must be eternal, immaterial, and immutable. The unmoved mover is not merely the first in a series of movers or causes. Aristotle realized that if the unmoved mover were merely the first mover, this would require that something else moved it. Similarly, if the unmoved mover were the first cause, this would require that something else caused it.

Aristotle understood that, to escape the illogical morass of infinite regress, the ultimate cause of motion must be an uncaused cause or an unmoved mover. Actuality must *precede* potentiality, just as being must precede becoming. Therefore being precedes becoming by logical necessity. This forms the classical root for the notion that "God" is a logically necessary being, an *ens necessarium*. Later philosophical theology would add that God is necessary not only logically but also ontologically. That is, pure being has its power of being within itself. It is self-existent and cannot *not* be.

Aristotle's "god" did not rise to the level of the Judaeo-Christian God. It remained a kind of impersonal force. Aristotle had no doctrine of creation. Rather, the unmoved mover is the ultimate form of eternal matter, which moves the world not by force but by attraction, as a light draws a moth to itself. This power of attraction then becomes also the efficient cause that "moves" things in this world. And, the unmoved mover is the *final* directing of all things to their proper end, their ultimate teleological purpose. It is ultimate thought that does not contemplate the world and offers no intelligent providence. It is pure thought thinking itself.

Aristotle's understanding of God did influence the later thinking of Thomas Aquinas, but it would be a mistake to assume an identity between the god of Aristotle and the God of Aquinas.

Will Durant once likened Aristotle's unmoved mover to the king of England. Aristotle's god, said Durant, is like a "do-nothing king" who "reigns but . . . does not rule."[2]

4

Augustine: Doctor of Grace

If Western civilization was "saved" from disintegrating into barbarianism by Socrates, Plato, and Aristotle, it may be said that the advent of Christianity and Christian philosophy had a similarly salutary effect.

The golden age of Greece began to tarnish after the death of Aristotle, and it soon turned to rust with later philosophical movements. As the metaphysical impasse of Heraclitus and Parmenides yielded an era of skepticism and Sophism, so the impasse of Plato and Aristotle led to a new wave of philosophical skepticism.

The only two philosophical schools mentioned by name in the New Testament are the Stoics and the Epicureans, whom the apostle Paul encountered at the Areopagus in Athens (Acts 17:18). The Stoics and Epicureans were rival schools founded at about the same time, around 300 B.C. Stoicism was founded by Zeno of Citium and Epicureanism by Epicurus.

Though both schools eschewed the rising skepticism that followed in Aristotle's wake, they clearly departed in focus and emphasis from the metaphysical quest for ultimate reality.

The Stoics

The Stoics developed a cosmology of materialism. They emphasized Heraclitus's view of the seminal fire that determines all things, the *logos spermatikos*. This universal *logos* produces seeds or "sparks," the *logoi spermatikoi,* in all things, so that every person has within himself a spark of the divine.

The central concern of Stoicism was moral philosophy. Virtue is found in one's response to materialistic determinism. Man cannot determine his own fate. He has no control over what happens to him. His freedom is restricted to his inner response or attitude to what befalls him. The goal of a virtuous life is philosophical *ataraxia,* a goal the Stoics shared in common with the Epicureans.

What is ataraxia? The word is rarely heard in the English language, save as the name of a tranquilizer. This Greek word may loosely be translated "peace of mind" or "tranquility of the soul." Though both Stoics and Epicureans sought ataraxia, they differed sharply on how to attain it.

Stoics sought ataraxia through practicing "imperturbability," the acceptance of one's lot with serenity and courage. Their theme song could have been "Qué será, será," "What will be, will be." The wise person finds virtue in strength of will. The secret of a good and happy life is the knowledge of what is under our control and what is not. Socrates was a heroic model to Stoics by virtue of the serenity with which he faced his execution. Later, Epictetus said, "I cannot escape death, but cannot I escape the dread of it?"[1]

The views of the ancient Stoics constitute what we now describe as a stoical attitude toward life, the philosophy of the "stiff upper lip," by which nothing ever rattles us or causes us to despair. When one perfects the practice of imperturbability, the soul remains in a state of tranquil bliss.

The Epicureans

The Epicureans, on the other hand, rejected a materialistic determinism and affirmed a much broader scope for human freedom.

They were hostile to religion, because they believed that religion engenders a superstitious, debilitating fear. They saw philosophy as humanely liberating people from their bondage to religion.

Epicureans sought ataraxia through what I call "refined hedonism," as opposed to crass or crude forms of hedonism. Refined hedonism defines the good as the attainment of pleasure and avoidance of pain.

The ancient Cyrenaics were an example of crude hedonism. They were gluttons, seeking physical pleasure to the maximum degree. The Cyrenaic idea was exhibited in Hollywood movies depicting ancient orgies and feasts in which people gorged themselves on food and wine, induced vomiting by sticking their fingers down their throats, then gorged themselves again. The Cyrenaics satiated themselves with food, drink, and sex, seeking to gratify every lust and satisfy every physical appetite.

Unlike the Cyrenaics, the Epicureans sought a refined and sophisticated enjoyment of pleasure by indulging themselves in moderation. Theirs was no simplistic formula of, "Eat, drink, and be merry, for tomorrow we die." They understood that there are different kinds of pleasure—pleasures of the mind as well as those of the body. Some pleasures are intense but short-lived. A preoccupation with intense and merely physical pleasure leads inevitably to two things one wants to avoid: unhappiness and pain. The goal for the Epicurean is not the intoxication that leads inevitably to a hangover but the absence of bodily pain and the presence of peace of mind, or ataraxia.

Epicureans sought to escape the "hedonistic paradox": The pursuit of pleasure alone ends in either frustration (if the pursuit fails) or boredom (if it succeeds). Both frustration and boredom are kinds of pain, the antithesis of pleasure. Thus Epicureans sought not the *maximum* pleasure but the *optimum* pleasure. They concluded that a wise man's diet of bread and water will more likely bring happiness than a glutton's diet of gourmet food.

The Skeptics

The post-Aristotelian revival of skepticism may be traced to Pyrrho and Arcesilaus, who founded two schools, Pyrrhonism and academic skepticism, respectively.

The skeptics cast doubt on the work of both Plato and Aristotle. Arcesilaus, who became the head of Plato's Academy in the third century B.C., rejected Plato's metaphysical philosophy. Arcesilaus denied that truth can be obtained with certainty, creating instead a philosophy of probability.

Skepticism was codified by Sextus Empericus around 200 B.C. He argued that for every philosophical proposition, a counter proposition of equal weight and force may be argued (anticipating to some degree the "antinomies" of Immanuel Kant in the modern period). The skeptics did not abandon the pursuit of truth. Indeed they pursued it vigorously. They tended, however, to remain aloof from any conclusions. They reflected the biblical description of those who are ever pursuing truth but never arrive at it (2 Tim. 3:7). They preferred not to reach firm conclusions, believing that the pursuit of truth cannot go that far. They were particularly cautious about drawing conclusions from sense perceptions, because the senses are so easily deceived. They also cast doubt on moral axioms, preferring to suspend judgment on ethical questions. Dogma was their enemy.

Though skepticism initially did influence Augustine's quest for truth, there were primarily two other major forces that reshaped the intellectual climate of the centuries immediately preceding him. The first, of course, was the advent of Christianity. The early Christian church turned the world upside down, and in an amazingly short span of time Christianity supplanted Greek philosophy as the dominant worldview. The Greeks did not surrender without a fight, however. Neoplatonism, the second major force, arose and presented a formidable challenge to Christianity.

The Neoplatonists

Plotinus (A.D. 204–270) was from Egypt, where he was exposed to the theories of the ancient Greeks as well as to Hellenistic Judaism and Christianity. He moved to Rome at the age of forty and consciously sought to develop a philosophy that would provide an alternative to Christianity. He wanted to revive Platonism, but to modify it so that it addressed the major issue introduced by Christian thought: salvation. His philosophy was eclectic and syncretistic, borrowing elements from various philosophers. He rejected the materialism of the Stoics and Epicureans, Aristotle's form-matter schema, and the Judaeo-Christian doctrine of creation.

Central to Neoplatonism is God, whom Plotinus calls "the One." In the final analysis, says Plotinus, all reality flows out of or emanates from the One. The One does not create, however, because creation would involve the One in an act of change. Rather, the world emanates by necessity from the One, in a way analogous to the rays of the sun emanating from its core. Reality is structured in layers or modes emanating from the One. The farther reality moves away from the core of the One, the more material that reality becomes.

Plotinus is often seen as a kind of pantheist, since he believes that all reality is ultimately a mode of the One. Yet he insists on a kind of transcendence for the One, which is higher in pure being than its subordinate modes of being. The first level of ema-

Table 4.1
Aristotle's Successors

	Birth–death (approx.)	Place of birth	Primary place of residence	Philosophy	Major work
Zeno	334–262 B.C.	Citium, Cyprus	Athens	Stoicism	*Republic*
Epicurus	341–271 B.C.	Samos	Athens	Epicureanism	*On Nature*
Pyrrho	365–275 B.C.		Elis, Greece	Pyrrhonism	
Arcesilaus	316–240 B.C.	Pitane, Asia Minor	Athens	Academic skepticism	
Sextus Empericus	Late 3d cent.–early 2d cent. B.C.			Skepticism	*Outlines of Pyrrhonism*
Plotinus	A.D. 204–270		Rome	Neo-platonism	*Enneads*

nation is the level of *nous or mind*, which is eternal and beyond time. Here is the Platonic realm of ideas. Out of *nous* comes the realm of the soul, and out of that comes the realm of matter, the lowest stage.

The One itself is ineffable. It cannot be grasped by reason or perceived by the senses. It is "known" only by mystical intuition or apprehension. No positive attribute can be assigned to it; it can be described only through the "way of negation" or the *via negationes*. That is, we can say about God only what he is not.

This method of negation functions to some degree in Christian theology. Although Christianity also has a "way of affirmation," it does employ the way of negation when it describes God as infinite (not finite), immutable (not mutable), uncreated (not created), and so forth.

The Doctor of Grace

We have taken a brief reconnaissance over the important movements of philosophy between the eras of Aristotle and Augustine so that we might better understand the weighty issues with which Augustine grappled.

Augustine was born in A.D. 354 in the town of Thagaste in Numidia (in present-day Algeria). His father was a pagan and his mother, Monica, a devout Christian. Augustine died in A.D. 430 after distinguishing himself as the supreme "doctor of grace." He was the greatest Christian philosopher-theologian of the first millennium and arguably of the entire Christian era.

As a young man Augustine displayed an extraordinary zeal for knowledge. After reading Cicero at age nineteen, Augustine dedicated his life to the pursuit of truth. He went through distinct periods of growth and upheaval. Initially he rejected Christianity and embraced the dualistic philosophy of Manichaeanism. Later he embraced skepticism and then went through a period of Neoplatonism. In 386 he experienced conversion to Christianity. Within ten years of his conversion, he became a bishop, a role he maintained until his death. His writings were voluminous, including the famous *Confessions* and *The City of God*.[2] He championed Christian orthodoxy in fierce theological struggles with heretics in the Donatist and Pelagian controversies.

It is said that Augustine achieved a philosophical synthesis between Platonism and Christianity, but his work did not set forth a system as such. His reflections on key areas of epistemology, creation, the problem of evil, and the nature of free will are of abiding importance. He influenced the development of the doctrine of the church, the doctrine of the Trinity, and the doctrine of grace in salvation.

Augustine combated all ancient forms of skepticism, seeking

to establish a foundation for truth. He sought truth within the mind or the soul, becoming the father of psychological introspection. He sought truth that was not merely probable but eternal, immutable, and independent. He was aware of the limitations of sensory knowledge and of the propensity for the senses to deceive us, which he illustrated by the example of a boat oar: From the eye's perspective an oar in the water is bent, but in reality the oar is straight.

Augustine searched for areas of certainty and discovered them in the realm of the rational and mathematical, as well as in self-consciousness. In the act of self-consciousness, the mind's objective reality is immediately known with certainty. Long before René Descartes posited his famous maxim, *Cogito, ergo sum* ("I think, therefore I am"), Augustine had formulated the argument. He countered the academic skeptics' fear of error and their probabilism by saying, "If I err, I am." He argued that a person who does not exist cannot err. Therefore, even if a person errs he cannot err without first existing. So even error proves the certainty of existence.

Augustine also argued that the law of noncontradiction cannot be disputed, for it must be assumed and employed in every effort to deny it. Thus, to deny the law of noncontradiction, or to "contradict" this law, is in fact to affirm it.

Augustine saw mathematics as a source of objective and indubitable truth. Like logic, math is not dependent on sensory data to establish its truth. Not only are two plus three equal to five, but two plus three will always equal five under any conditions.

Truth and Revelation

The concept of divine revelation was central to Augustine's epistemology, or theory of knowledge. He saw that revelation is the necessary condition for all knowledge. As Plato argued that to escape the shadows on the cave wall the prisoner must see things in the light of day, so Augustine argued that the light of divine revelation is necessary for knowledge.

The metaphor of light is instructive. In our present earthly state we are equipped with the faculty of sight. We have eyes, optic nerves, and so forth—all the equipment needed for seeing. But a man with the keenest eyesight can see nothing if he is locked in a totally dark room. So just as an external source of light is needed for seeing, so an external revelation from God is needed for knowing.

When Augustine speaks of revelation, he is not speaking of biblical revelation alone. He is also concerned with "general" or "natural" revelation. Not only are the truths found in Scripture dependent on God's revelation, but all truth, including scientific truth, is dependent on divine revelation. This is why Augustine encouraged students to learn as much as possible about as many things as possible. For him, all truth is God's truth, and when one encounters truth, one encounters the God whose truth it is.

Even in the act of self-awareness or self-consciousness, one is immediately aware of God. When I become aware of myself, I am at the same time aware of my finitude and of the God who made me. For Augustine, the knowledge of self and the knowledge of God are the twin goals of philosophy. As Augustine's disciple John Calvin later reflected, there is a mutually dependent, symbiotic relationship between the knowledge of God and the knowledge of self. I cannot know God until I am first aware of myself in thought, yet I cannot truly know myself except in relationship to God.

Augustine further argued the premise that Calvin would later call the *sensus divinitatis,* the immediate knowledge of God innate in the human soul. All people know that God exists, though not

all people will acknowledge that they know him. Their primal
sin is their refusal to honor God as God by refusing to acknowledge what they know to be true. People's ignorance about God's
existence is willful and therefore sinful ignorance.

Knowledge and Faith

Faith, says Augustine, is an essential ingredient of knowledge.
Augustine does not restrict his notion of faith to what we typically
refer to as religious faith. Faith also involves a provisional belief
in things before we can validate them through demonstration.
He adopted the famous motto *Credo ut intelligam*, "I believe in
order to understand."

In this sense faith is prior to reason. All knowledge begins in
faith. As children we accept what we are taught by faith. We
believe our parents and teachers until we can test what they say
for ourselves. We may doubt our parents' warning that the stove
is hot, but we demonstrate its truth by touching the stove ourselves.

We begin learning by provisional trust or faith. At this point
Augustine is careful to note the difference between faith and
credulity. Though in one sense faith is prior to reason, in another
sense reason is prior to faith. I cannot believe something that is
manifestly irrational. Knowledge, to be believed, must be intelligible. This does not preclude the realm of mystery, but there is a
big difference between a mystery and a contradiction.

I may not be able to plumb the depths of the mystery of gravity or motion, but it is not absurd to believe that gravity and
motion are real. Likewise, I may not have a comprehensive understanding of the mystery of the Trinity, but the concept of the
Trinity is not contradictory or irrational. I believe the truth of
the Trinity because I am convinced that it is revealed by divine rev-

elation, to which I, on sane and sober grounds, yield an implicit faith *(fides implicitum)*. If, for example, I know that God exists and is omniscient and wholly righteous, I would be foolish to doubt what he clearly reveals.

To Augustine faith is not, like credulity, blind or arbitrary. To be credulous is to believe the absurd or irrational—to believe without good reason. Right faith for Augustine is always a reasonable faith. Revelation yields information that one cannot gain by unaided reason, but never information that is opposed to the laws of reason.

Creation

Over against Greek philosophy, Augustine staunchly defended the biblical concept of creation. God's work of creation, said Augustine, is voluntary and purposive. Creation is not of necessity (as in Greek thought), nor is the material world eternal. The universe had a beginning. There was a "time" when the universe was not. I put *time* in quotation marks because time is a corollary of space and matter. When asked by skeptics what God was doing before he created the world, Augustine replied, "Creating hell for curious souls!"

According to Augustine, God created all things *ex nihilo,* "out of nothing." Augustine was not violating the maxim *Ex nihilo, nihil fit,* "Out of nothing, nothing comes." He did not argue that once there was nothing and suddenly there was something. This notion of self-creation is irrational, and only the credulous affirm it. For something to create itself, it must exist before it existed, a manifest violation of the law of noncontradiction, as the thing must *be* and *not be* at the same time and in the same relationship. Before creating the world, the eternal God existed, so creation *ex nihilo* does not mean creation *by* nothing. Using

Aristotle's view of causality, we may say that the universe had a formal, final, and efficient cause, but not a *material* cause.

Since God is good, all that he originally created was good. That which is material is not, as in Platonism, inherently evil. However, although the universe, including man, was created by God, he did not make it *immutably* good. The present world is fallen.

The Problem of Evil

Wrestling with the problem of evil, Augustine sought to define evil in purely negative terms. Evil is a lack, privation *(privatio)*, or negation *(negatio)* of the good. Only that which was first good can become evil. Evil is defined against the backdrop of the prior concept of the good. Evil depends on the good for its very definition. We speak of evil in terms of *un*righteousness, *in*justice, and law*less*ness. The Antichrist depends on Christ for his very identity. As a parasite depends on its host for its existence, so evil depends on the good for its existence. Anything that participates in being, so far that it exists, is good. Nonexistence is evil. If anything were purely or totally evil, it could not exist. Evil is not a substance or a thing. It is a lack or privation of the good.

At this level Augustine seems to be defining evil in purely ontological terms. If this were the case, Augustine would have to say that evil is a necessary consequence of finitude. God cannot create an ontologically "perfect" being. To do so would be to create another God. Even God cannot create another God, because the second God would be, by definition, a creature.

To avoid the ontological necessity of evil, Augustine turned to free will. God created man with a free will *(liberum arbitrium)*, in which he also enjoyed perfect liberty *(libertas)*. Man had the faculty of choosing what he wanted. He had the ability to sin *(posse peccare)* and the ability not to sin *(posse non peccare).* He freely chose to sin out of his concupiscence (an inclination that leans to sin but is not sin).

As a result of the first sin, man lost his liberty but not his free will. He was plunged, as a divine punishment, into a corrupt state known as original sin, losing the ability to incline himself to the things of God. This resulted in man's absolute dependence on a work of divine grace in his soul if he were ever to move toward God. Fallen man is in bondage to sin. He still has the faculty of choosing, a will free from coercion, but he now is free only to sin, because his desires are inclined only toward sin and away from God. Now *posse non peccare,* "the ability not to sin," is lost and in its place is *non posse non peccare,* "the *in*ability not to sin." With this view Augustine combated the heretic Pelagius, who denied original sin. Pelagius argued that Adam's sin affected Adam alone and that all people have the ability to live perfect lives.

Augustine remains a patron saint of the Roman Catholic Church, but he was also claimed by Protestantism's magisterial leaders, Martin Luther and John Calvin, as their chief theological mentor.

Table 4.2
Humanity as Created and Fallen

	Humanity as created	Fallen humanity	Latin term
Free will	yes	yes	*liberum arbitrium*
Liberty	yes	no	*libertas*
The ability to sin	yes	yes	*posse peccare*
The ability not to sin	yes	no	*posse non peccare*
The *in*ability not to sin	no	yes	*non posse non peccare*

Thomas Aquinas: Angelic Doctor

The apex of intellectual accolades is to be known merely by one's last name. Titles such as doctor or professor are dropped, and usually first names are bypassed. We do not need to know that Descartes' first name was René or that Hume's first name was David. But in the case of Aquinas this all changes. To cite this prodigious scholar one need refer only to his first name, Thomas. Indeed, his thought is often referred to simply as Thomism.

The Catholic Church not only canonized Thomas but conferred on him the honorific title "Doctor Angelicus." The angelic doctor stands as a giant in the intellectual world, and his work continues to be studied in every university, both sacred and secular. The great theologians of history display different styles and different gifts. But for sheer weight of intellect, I doubt that Thomas has had any peers, unless it is the Puritan divine Jonathan Edwards.

Thomas Aquinas was born in 1225 near Naples, Italy. His father, a count of Aquino, was of the aristocracy. At five years of age Thomas entered the Abbey of Monte Cassino, where he studied until enrolling at the University of Naples at age fourteen. While there he entered the Dominican Order, a group of friars devoted to teaching. From Naples Thomas went to the University of Paris at age eighteen. At the time the most heralded theologian in the world was Albert the Great (Albertus Magnus). Albert was known as "the universal teacher." As Plato had his Socrates and Aristotle his Plato, so Thomas had the benefit of the tutelage of Albert.

While studying under Albert, Thomas was ridiculed and teased by his classmates. They called him "the dumb ox of Aquino," provoking Albert to say that someday this dumb ox would astound the world. On one occasion a classmate gaped out a window and said, "Look, Thomas, there is a cow flying." Thomas got up from his seat and went to the window to see. His classmates broke into laughter at his naïveté. Thomas turned around and said, "I would rather believe that cows can fly than that one of my brothers would lie to me."

The dumb ox of Aquino went on to become the supreme force of scholastic philosophy and theology. Samuel Stumpf refers to the scholastic period as the apex of medieval philosophy. In modern times *scholasticism* has become a pejorative term. We live in perhaps the most anti-intellectual period of Christian history. We affirm technology and education, but we demean the role of the mind or intellect, particularly in the religious realm. Scholastic thinkers appear to us dry and arid. They seem to lack creativity, and we dismiss their abstract reasoning as desultory debates about how many angels can dance on the head of a pin. (The fundamentalist is not concerned about such questions, because he is quite sure that angels don't dance!)

Scholastic philosophy sought to create a coherent and comprehensive system of thought. Scholastics became experts at systemic thinking. They were not so much concerned with vignettes of thought or with novel ideas. Rather, they sought to codify traditional thought into a cogent system (the "anti-system" sentiment found in modern existential philosophy has biased many against this approach to truth).

Scholastic philosophers relied heavily on rigorous logic, emphasizing the art of deductive reasoning. To express their ideas

Table 5.1
Four Men Who Changed the World

	Years of birth–death	Place of birth	Primary place of residence	Mentor	Position
Plato	428–348 B.C.	Greece	Athens	Socrates	Founder of the Academy
Aristotle	384–322 B.C.	Thrace, Macedonia	Athens	Plato	Head of Lyceum
Augustine	A.D. 354–430	Thagaste, Numidia	Hippo, Numidia	Ambrose of Milan	Bishop of Hippo
Thomas Aquinas	A.D. 1225–1274	Aquino, Italy	Paris	Albert the Great	Professor

they favored the method of disputation. Anyone who has read deeply in the works of Thomas Aquinas is struck by the absence of voluminous footnotes and the sheer force of supporting a thesis by vigorous argument alone. In this tradition Thomas emerged as the undisputed master.

Perhaps no Roman Catholic thinker has been more maligned, misunderstood, and misrepresented by Protestant critics, especially evangelical critics, than has Thomas. It is widely accepted that Thomas's most egregious error was to separate nature and grace. This charge is unmitigated nonsense; nothing could be further from the truth. To charge Thomas with separating nature from grace is to miss the primary thrust of his entire philosophy, particularly with respect to his monumental defense of the Christian faith.

Nature and Grace

It is crystal clear that Thomas makes a sharp distinction between nature and grace. What must be noted at this point, however, is that one of the most important philosophical distinctions is the distinction between a distinction and a separation. For example, in theology we distinguish between Christ's human and divine natures, all the while realizing that the two natures exist in perfect unity and that to separate them is to commit the Nestorian heresy. To make the point perhaps more graphically, I have done you no harm if I *distinguish* between your body and your soul. If I *separate* your body from your soul, however, I have murdered you.

Thomas's distinction between nature and grace was designed not to separate them but to demonstrate their ultimate unity and connection. It was precisely against the idea of separating them that Thomas strove so mightily. He was keenly aware of the growing threat to Christianity from Islam. Islamic philosophers had already experienced their own renaissance through rediscovering classical Greek thought. Principal thinkers such as Averroës had already synthesized Muslim theology and Aristotle's philosophy. Their work was known as "integral Aristotelianism" because they had integrated Aristotle with Islam.

These Muslim philosophers constructed a "double truth" theory, arguing that what is true in faith may be false in reason, what is true in philosophy may be false in theology, what is true in religion may be false in science, and vice versa. This intellectual schizophrenia separates nature and grace with a vengeance. It would be analogous to a modern Christian saying that from the vantage point of faith (grace), man is created by God in his image and for a purpose, a being with dignity because God has bestowed it on him; but that from the vantage point of reason (nature), man is a cosmic accident, a grown-up germ who emerged from the primordial slime and is destined for annihilation, a being with no dignity whatever. This confused believer affirms macroevolution from Monday to Saturday, but on Sunday worships the God of creation.

Thomas is credited with achieving the "classical synthesis"

between philosophy and theology. We recall the idea that in the medieval university theology was queen of the sciences and philosophy was her handmaiden. Thomas is seen as producing a synthesis of Aristotelian philosophy and Christian theology in a fashion similar to Augustine's producing a synthesis of Platonic philosophy and Christian theology. This view of Thomas can easily be overstated, because he was sharply critical of many elements of Aristotelian philosophy (particularly the ones incorporated into integral Aristotelianism). The difference between Augustine and Thomas is also often overstated. Even a cursory reading of Thomas's *Summa Theologica*[1] reveals that in many respects Thomas stood on Augustine's shoulders.

Thomas believed that philosophy and theology play complementary roles in the quest for truth. Grace does not destroy nature but fulfills it. Thomas saw clear boundaries between the two disciplines but found both necessary to understand reality comprehensively.

Thomas believed in the primacy of divine revelation. He did not, as many have charged, see nature as functioning independently of revelation. He based his so-called "natural theology" on natural revelation. Just as Protestant theologians distinguish between general (or natural) revelation and special (biblical) revelation, so Thomas distinguishes between nature and grace. In his discussion of nature and grace in *Summa Theologica,* Thomas roots his thought in the apostle Paul's view of God's self-revelation in nature, as expressed in his letter to the Romans. In this same section Thomas labors the point that all knowledge, in both nature and grace, is dependent on the revelation of God. He quotes Augustine's analogy of our dependence on light for sight. This should dispel the idea that Thomas saw natural theology as a function of man's unaided reason. All knowledge rests and depends on God's revelation. This revelation, however, is not found exclusively in the Bible but shines through the cosmos as well.

Thomas maintained that some truths can be known only through the Scriptures, which are the chief venue of theology. One does not learn of God's plan of salvation by studying astronomy or astrology. Other truths, however, are found in nature but are not disclosed in Scripture. For example, the circulatory system of the body and the behavioral patterns of photons can be discovered only by studying nature (that such discoveries attest to the grace of God, without whose benevolent providence they could not be known, Thomas would not dispute). Thus philosophy (and science) and theology comprise two distinct spheres of knowledge. Both are dependent on revelation, and they are complementary, not antithetical. For Thomas, all truth is God's truth and all truth meets at the top.

Thomas's view of natural theology encounters its greatest opposition from fideists (who argue that God is known only by faith) in his view of the "mixed articles" *(articulus mixtus)*. These are truths that can be learned by either nature *or* grace—by either philosophy or science, or from the Bible. This class of mixed articles includes the knowledge of the existence of God. This means that philosophy, apart from the Bible, can rationally demonstrate God's existence. Of course the Bible affords a much broader and deeper knowledge of God's character, says Thomas, but his actual existence can be demonstrated apart from the Bible. With respect to the knowledge of God, philosophy and theology can work together as partners.

Proofs of God's Existence

Departing from Anselm's earlier ontological proof of the existence of God, which proceeds from the idea of God's existence to his

Table 5.2
The Source of Our Knowledge of Truth

Kinds of truth	Theological truth	Philosophical, scientific truth	"Mixed articles"
Sphere	Grace	Nature	Grace or nature
Example	God's plan of salvation	The body's circulatory system	God's existence
Immediate source	The Bible	The natural world	The Bible or the natural world
Ultimate source	God: his special revelation	God: his general revelation	God: his special or general revelation

actual existence, Thomas works more from a cosmological framework, reasoning from the cosmos back to God.

The *first proof* Thomas offers is the proof from motion. He begins with the evidence for motion in the world (Zeno notwithstanding). Borrowing heavily from Aristotle, Thomas argues that whatever is moved is moved by another (based on what we call the law of inertia). Thomas defines motion as the reduction of something from potentiality to actuality. An object at rest may have the potential to move, but it does not move until or unless this potential is actualized. But, Thomas argues, nothing can be reduced from potentiality to actuality except by something that is already in a state of actuality. For example, fire can make a piece of wood, which is only potentially hot, actually hot. Something cannot be at the same time both actual and potential. What is actually hot may be at the same time potentially cold, but it cannot be potentially hot while it is actually hot. It could be potentially hotter than it actually is, but to become hotter it must be moved to that state. Whatever is moved must be moved by some prior actuality. But this change cannot regress to infinity, because in that case the motion could never begin. Therefore, Thomas concludes, there must be a first mover, and everyone understands this to be God.

Thomas's *second proof* is the proof from efficient cause. The law of causality asserts that every effect must have an antecedent cause. This is not the same thing as saying that every *thing* must have a cause (as John Stuart Mill and Bertrand Russell claim). If every *thing* must have a cause, then God himself would require a cause. The law of causality refers only to effects and is an extension of the law of noncontradiction. The law is formally true, because it is true by definition. An effect is defined as that which is produced by a cause. An effect cannot be an effect unless it has a cause. Likewise, a cause (properly speaking) is by definition that which produces an effect. A cause cannot be a cause unless it causes or produces something. An uncaused (self-existent) being violates no rule of reason; an uncaused effect, however, is irrational and absurd.

In Aristotle's scheme the efficient cause is that which produces the effect. In the case of the statue, it is the sculptor. Without the sculptor there will be no statue because there is nothing to cause it. No event can be its own cause. Every event requires a prior cause. Any change in anything is an event. Every prior cause must have its own cause (if the prior event is itself an effect). At some point the series must end. It is impossible to regress to infinity, as the idea of an infinite regress involves the notion of a causeless effect, an absurdity infinitely compounded.

Thomas Aquinas's *third proof* of God's existence is the proof from necessary being *(ens necessarium)*. Although this is usually thought of as part of the cosmological argument, it is more properly called "ontological," because it is an argument from being. In nature we find things that are *contingent,* things that can be or not be (a possibility Hamlet fully understood about himself). Such things or "beings" do not always exist. They also experience the changes involved in generation and decay. There was a time when I was not. To say that it is possible for something not to exist can mean that once in the past it did not exist, that it can go out of existence in the future (at least as an individuated entity), or both. Possible being then refers to beings that possibly can *not be.*

No merely possible being is self-existent; it does not have the power of being in itself. If all things in reality were only *possible,* then at one time there would have been nothing in existence. If there was a time when nothing existed, then nothing could ever start to exist and nothing would exist now. But if something *does* exist now, there must have always been something in existence; something must exist that possesses *necessary* existence—its existence is not merely possible but necessary. It cannot *not* be. It does not receive its existence from something else. There never was a time when it was not. In other words, if anything exists now, then something must have the power of being within itself, that is, something must have necessary being. This being, whose being is both logically and ontologically necessary, is God.

Thomas's *fourth proof* is the proof from degrees of perfection, in which he borrows heavily from Augustine. This is an argument from the comparative. We are aware of degrees of the good, the true, and the noble. But something can be deemed good or true only against some maximum norm or standard. Modern relativists posit truths with no truth, goods with no good, virtues with no virtue, and purposes with no purpose. But we cannot have a relative of anything unless the relative is measured against an absolute. Thomas argues that the maximum in any genus is the cause of everything in that genus. For example, fire, which is the maximum of heat, is the cause of all hot things. There must also be something which is to all beings the cause of their being, goodness, and every other perfection, and this we call God.

It could be counter-argued that if this is true, then God would

also have to be maximally or perfectly evil—to account for the relative degrees of evil in the world. This is why it was crucial to
Thomas, following Augustine, to define evil by way of privation
and negation. The ultimate standard by which we must judge
evil is not maximum evil but maximum perfection.

Thomas's *fifth* and final *proof* of God's existence proceeds
from the evidence of order in the universe. This is a form of the so-
called teleological argument. The term *teleological* comes from the
Greek *telos,* which means "end, purpose, or goal."

In nature we observe things that lack intelligence but function in an orderly and purposive way. They act in predictable ways
to achieve certain ends or functions. The seeds of a dandelion
cast in the wind are designed for the plant's reproduction. These
things appear to act with a purpose. One cannot have purpose
accidentally, nor can one have unintentional intentionality. In its
simplest form the teleological argument rests on the evidence of
design in the universe. Design demands a designer, an idea that
deeply impressed both Immanuel Kant and David Hume despite
their skepticism.

Thomas argues that things lacking intelligence (note in this
word the root *telos*) cannot act in a designed fashion unless they
are first directed by something that does have intelligence. An
arrow does not guide itself to the target unless it is first aimed there
by the archer. "Smart bombs" are not really smart unless pro-
grammed by someone who is smart (and even then, they are not
always so smart!).

Aquinas concludes that there must be an intelligent being who
directs all natural things to their end. This he calls God. It must
be added that things cannot be directed to their ends by chance.
Chance can direct nothing, because chance can do nothing.
Chance can do nothing because chance is nothing. *Chance* is a
perfectly meaningful term to describe mathematical possibilities,

but the word becomes a sneaky bogeyman when used to describe something that has the power to influence anything. Chance has no being, and that which has no being has no power to do anything.[2]

In developing his natural theology, Thomas uses qualifying terms to describe the knowledge of God that we can draw from nature. He says our knowledge of God from nature, while true, is mediate, analogous, and incomplete.

When Thomas Aquinas speaks of *mediate* knowledge, he is distinguishing it from immediate knowledge. If something is said to be known "immediately" in this sense, this does not mean that it is known instantly or quickly (though it may be). This means instead that it is known directly and not through some medium. When I watch a basketball game on television, I am watching action that is taking place miles away, where I am not immediately present. I am really watching an electronically transmitted picture of the game. I am watching the game through the medium of television. (The *media* are called *media* because they stand between us and the actual events they report.)

Thomas calls natural theology "mediate" because God's revelation comes to us through the medium of creation. The heavens declare the glory of God in that God reveals his glory through the heavens. In this regard the apostle Paul declared in Romans that God is known through "the things that are made" (Rom. 1:20).

When Thomas says that natural theology is *analogous,* he is speaking of a function of language. He discerns three ways in which language functions: univocal, equivocal, and analogical. With univocal language a word means basically the same thing when applied to different beings. With equivocal language the meaning of a term changes dramatically when applied to two different beings. Consider, for example, the word *bald.* If I speak of a bald man, I mean that the man lacks hair on his head. If, how-

ever, I criticize a dramatic reading by saying that the oral inter-
preter gave a "bald narrative," I do not mean that the narrative
was hairless; I mean that the narrative lacked something, such as
passion, expressiveness, or pizzazz.

With analogical language, the meaning of a term changes
proportionally when two different beings are described. For
example, when I say that my dog is a good dog, I do not mean that
he actively pursues virtue and has a highly sensitized conscience.
Rather I mean that he comes when I call him, is house-broken, and
does not bite the mailman on the leg. Conversely, when I say that
a man is good, I do not mean that he comes when I call him, is
house-broken, and does not bite the mailman on the leg. Man's
capacity for goodness exceeds that of a dog, so the term *good* is
used proportionately or analogically to man.

When Thomas Aquinas says that our knowledge of God is
analogous, he means that our language about God falls short of
describing him exactly. God is infinite and we are finite. We are
different from God, but not so different that our language about
him is meaningless or merely equivocal. It is meaningful because
it is analogical. Analogical language about God is possible because
there is some sense in which man resembles God. This is what
Thomas calls the *analogia entis,* the "analogy of being," between
man and God. This analogy of being is rooted in man's having
been created in God's image.

Modern theologians such as Karl Barth unleashed an assault
on Thomas's concept of the analogy of being, an assault that back-
fired with the "death of God" movement. Thomas understood that
if God were "wholly other" or totally dissimilar to us (as Barth
claimed), then we would have no way at all to speak about God.

The *incompleteness* of our knowledge of God from natural
theology does not make this knowledge worthless. Critics of
Thomistic natural theology often complain that the God known

through nature is at best an unmoved mover and is not the God of the Bible. Yet even the biblical revelation of God is neither exhaustive nor comprehensive. To say that God is not known fully or even redemptively through natural theology is not to say he is not known at all. Aquinas argues that, despite the fact that natural theology is mediate, analogous, and incomplete, it is nevertheless true as far as it goes. There is great value to theology and especially to apologetics to demonstrate that God is self-existent and eternal. For example, though God is more than self-existent, he is by no means less than self-existent. It is also crucial to see that most of the debate over theism in our day focuses on the issue of creation, a doctrine that is powerfully defended by the proof of God's self-existence and necessary being.

René Descartes:
Father of Modern Rationalism

Between Thomas Aquinas's classical synthesis in the thirteenth century and the dawn of the Age of Reason in the seventeenth, dramatic changes altered the landscape of Western civilization. Changes in religion, political theory, science, and economic structure left the medieval world in ruins.

The Renaissance in Italy saw an attempt to revive ancient philosophy as a tool not only to foster religious concerns but also to allow philosophy a certain independence from theology. Lorenzo the Magnificent of the Medici family created the New Academy in Florence. With the revival of ancient philosophy came both a new Platonism and a new Stoicism, as well as a revival of ancient Pyrrhonic skepticism. The works of Sextus Empiricus were translated in the sixteenth century. The new skepticism asserted that claims to objective truth are prone to incite endless disputes and even warfare. These skeptics replaced objective truth with the logical principle of equipollence.

Equipollence was a deliberate technique of balancing any particular proposition with its contradictory counterpart. Every proposition has its antithesis, so each proposition's truth value is equally probable and improbable. This schema forces the philosopher to suspend judgment.

The skeptics argued particularly against knowledge of God,

assuming that our senses cannot apprehend being directly. We can only know the "appearance" of things, not their real being. This was once more a retreat into Plato's cave, with philosophers rolling a stone in front of its entrance. This skepticism was phenomenalism to a radical degree. *Phenomena,* as we have seen, refers to those things that are evident or manifest to our senses. According to phenomenalism, it is impossible to get behind or beyond the phenomena to reality.

In France some theologians welcomed the new skepticism because it liberated faith from reason. These Christian philosophers embraced a religious form of skepticism called fideistic skepticism. Montaigne, for example, argued that natural reason is incompetent to attain knowledge about being because it is totally dependent on the senses for the raw data on which the mind reflects. Any certainty about God's existence must come from religious faith alone.

With these developments theology, queen of the sciences, was divorced from her handmaiden philosophy. It was only a matter of time before the queen would be deposed from her throne altogether.

Other dramatic changes were also taking place. The world was growing smaller by means of the astonishing achievements of such explorers as Ferdinand Magellan and Vasco da Gama. West was meeting East, and the monolithic culture of the Middle Ages was being changed.

The Copernican Revolution

One of the most radical changes came by way of the new science. The sixteenth century witnessed not only the Protestant Reformation but also the Copernican revolution. For almost two millennia the Aristotelian worldview, as developed by Ptolemy in his *The Almagest,*[1] reigned virtually without challenge. Ptolemy's elaborate astronomical model of the heavens with its complex system of crystalline spheres "worked," affording scientists a model that enabled them to predict the movements of stars and planets. This ancient model viewed the earth as the center of the universe. The earth does not move, but the stars do. They are fixed on an invisible crystal "roof" that moves on its axis around the earth every day.

With the advent of the printing press, the writings of ancient thinkers became more widely distributed. Nicolaus Copernicus was one scientist who benefited by collecting a larger library of books. He particularly admired Ptolemy's *Almagest* and studied it closely. He was impressed by Ptolemy's accuracy but was bothered by inherent deficiencies in his work. After much deliberation Copernicus sought a more central truth concerning the shape of the universe. At the center of the universe he placed the sun, upsetting the medieval order by replacing geocentricity with heliocentricity.

Still committed to the ancient idea that the circle is the most perfect form, Copernicus conceived that the planets move in circular orbits. As a result, the model he set forth in his book *De Revolutionibus Orbium Caelestium (On the Revolution of Heavenly Spheres)*[2] worked little better than Ptolemy's model. Both Protestant and Catholic scholars railed against the new theory, seeing it as an attack on the Bible and human dignity. This world was no longer at the center of God's universe!

But the cat was out of the bag. Later astronomers, such as Giordano Bruno and Tycho Brahe, continued to develop the Copernican theory. Tycho's apprentice, Johannes Kepler, worked for eight years to solve the problem of the apparent retrograde motion of the planet Mars. He finally succeeded by discovering that the planet's orbit is not a circle but a perfect ellipse. By assum-

ing an elliptical motion of the planets, Kepler was able to make the
Copernican system work perfectly.

The Copernican theory was confirmed by the experiments of
Galileo Galilei and perhaps most astonishingly by Ferdinand
Magellan as he circumnavigated the globe. Magellan's sailors
discovered a discrepancy between the dates in their logbooks and
the dates in ports where they stopped (after crossing the interna-
tional dateline). This phenomenon proved that the earth is rotat-
ing on its axis.

In addition to the upheaval in science was the upheaval in religion known as the Protestant Reformation. During the sixteenth
century Martin Luther's view of *sola Scriptura* challenged the
absolute authority of the church, and Christendom was frag-
mented as never before. Protestants replaced papal and ecclesias-
tical authority with biblical authority, and the infallible Bible
alone could bind the believer's conscience.

A Born Mathematician

Into this milieu of theological, philosophical, and scientific
upheaval, René Descartes was born. Descartes, who has been called
the "father of modern philosophy," was born in 1596 in Touraine,
France. He studied mathematics, logic, and philosophy at the Jesuit
college of La Flèche. His chief discipline was mathematics.

Much of the scientific progress that had changed the world
had been spearheaded by advances in mathematics. It was the
quest for a more consistent and accurate mathematical model for
astronomy that drove the new Copernicans. It was the discoveries in the formal realm of mathematics that led to discoveries in
the material realm of the natural sciences. We recall that in a
sense mathematics is an extension of logic, a kind of symbolic
logic. In this realm of pure formal demonstration, the vagaries of

sense perception are overcome or transcended; this realm the skeptics could not overcome. No amount of equipollence could ever make three plus four equal anything but seven.

After traveling widely throughout Europe, Descartes settled in Holland in 1628. Here he penned his first work, *Discourse on Method,* in 1631.[3] Descartes was driven by a quest for certainty. Philosophy was in a state of confusion. Science was fussing with religion. The church was split between rival claims of authority. To achieve certainty amid such confusion, Descartes turned to math. He sought a system or method of thinking that emulates the mathematical model. In math the mind apprehends truth clearly and directly, making mathematical truth clear and distinct.

The twin pillars of the mathematical model are deduction and what Descartes calls intuition. Deductive reasoning moves from the universal to the particular, as opposed to inductive reasoning, which moves from the particular to the universal. Examining the following classic syllogism will illustrate the difference between deduction and induction:

Premise 1: All men are mortal.
Premise 2: Socrates is a man.
Conclusion: Therefore Socrates is mortal.

The first premise is a universal affirmative statement: All members of a class (men) have the attribute or predicate of mortality. The second premise is a particular affirmative: A particular individual (Socrates) belongs to the class of men. The conclusion (a particular affirmative) that Socrates is mortal is reached by logical certainty. By the law of immediate inference, if all members of a class possess a certain attribute, then a particular member of this class must also possess that attribute.

A syllogism is neither true nor false: It is either valid or invalid, depending on whether the conclusion flows from the premises. Only *statements* can be true or false. What logic measures is the relationship between statements or propositions. What the above syllogism proves *deductively* is this: If all men are mortal and if Socrates is a man, then it is indubitably and demonstrably true that Socrates is mortal.

Does this prove that Socrates is mortal? Not necessarily. That conclusion is true only if the premises of the syllogism are true. How do we know that all men are mortal? This universal premise is based on *induction*. If we know that every human being born before, say, 1850 has since died, we have a large sampling of particulars that manifest a common attribute, mortality. But suppose that the present generation of living people is the first generation of people who are immortal. Though this is highly unlikely, it is not theoretically impossible. Add to this that the number of people now alive is probably higher than the number of all people who were born before 1850, and we would see that after inductively studying less than half of all people, we have "jumped" to a conclusion about all of them.

But suppose a nuclear holocaust killed every person on earth except you. Then could you know inductively that all men are mortal? Not with absolute certainty. You might be the one exception that would refute the universal truth. The probability that you too are mortal would be almost certain, but it would not be absolutely certain. Your universal premise could be known to be true only if you also died and nobody was left. Only posthumously could you arrive at the absolute universal.

What about the second premise, that Socrates is a man? Perhaps Socrates was merely a figment of Plato's imagination. Perhaps he was a robot or an alien from outer space. These theoretical possibilities may be outrageous or outlandish in the extreme, but they remain, however remote and unlikely, philosophical possibilities. In this regard we see that inductive research can never achieve absolute formal certainty because it can never be exhaustive. Only formal truth (that which pertains to form or essence) can yield philosophical certitude.

Along with deduction Descartes sought intuitive knowledge. By intuition he does not mean some inner hunch or sentiment. He defines intuition as an intellectual activity of such clarity and distinctness that it leaves no doubt in the mind. One example of intuitive knowledge is that a triangle must have three sides.

In his *Discourse* Descartes sets forth four rules to be followed in quest of truth: 1) never accept as true anything that is not known to be true without doubt; 2) divide each difficulty under examination into as many parts as possible and necessary to solve it; 3) conduct thinking by commencing with objects that are the simplest and easiest to know, then ascend little by little to the more complex; 4) in every case make enumerations so complete and reviews so general that you might be assured you have omitted or overlooked nothing.

In a later, unfinished treatise Descartes expands his list. *Rules for the Direction of the Mind*[4] contains twenty-one rules, including this one: Direct your inquiries, not to what others have thought, nor to your own conjecture, but to what you can behold with clarity and deduce with certainty.

Descartes insists on thoroughgoing self-criticism. While engaged in the learning process, we assimilate ideas and theories galore, many of which we accept gratuitously and uncritically. We are vulnerable to "love lines" that tether us to family, friends, and affinity groups and that prejudice us in favor of their views. We must never assume something is true just because our favorite teacher espouses it or our parents taught us to believe it.

Descartes' method involves a relentless pursuit of fundamental truth that is so certain that everything else can be tested against it. He wants his primary truths so well established that he can crawl into his Dutch oven and deduce the rest without exposure to the external world.

To achieve these foundational, clear, and distinct ideas, Descartes establishes a rigorous process of systematic doubt that would make a skeptic envious. Descartes rejects as false anything about which he can imagine the slightest doubt. For example, how do I know that at this very minute I am putting words on a page with my pen? How do I know I am not simply dreaming that I am writing? He argues that there are no conclusive indicators by which one can distinguish waking life from sleep. (At times I myself am vexed by thorny questions about memory. I have had dreams so vivid and intense that years later I am not sure if I am remembering a dream or a real experience.)

Descartes is aware that our senses tend to deceive us. We remember Augustine's bent oar, or the experience of thirsty desert travelers who see mirages. If I see a man in the distance and then hold my thumb in front of me, the man appears to be no bigger than my thumbnail.

With respect to dreaming, Descartes falls back on mathematical certainty. Whether I am dreaming or awake, four plus three equals seven. But even this could be wrong if the universe is ruled by a malevolent God or devil who deceives me into thinking that four plus three equals seven.

Religious authorities disagree, says Descartes, so they cannot be the final arbiters of truth. At this point in his doubting process, Descartes is looking for at least one truth that is certain, one primary truth that can function as an indubitable first principle, a truth that is self-evident, a truth that will enable him to attain other truths.

If Descartes is known for anything, it is for his famous maxim *Cogito, ergo sum,* "I think, therefore I am." Whatever else

Descartes does not know, he knows for sure that he is a thinker or a being that thinks. To doubt the truth that I am thinking, I must think. I cannot doubt that I am thinking without affirming that I am thinking. To be thinking I must exist, because thought requires a thinker.

It must be noted that this first principle ("I think, therefore I am.") embraces at least two unspoken assumptions. The first is the law of noncontradiction. Part of the self-evident truth of Descartes' maxim is that one cannot think and not think at the same time and in the same relationship. This formal truth underlies the certainty of one's self-conscious existence. The second assumption is the law of causality. This formal truth yields the conclusion that thought requires a thinker.

The Existence of God

With his first principle, Descartes achieves certainty about his own existence. But what does this say about the existence of others, the existence of the world, and the existence of God? How can Descartes get beyond the limits of self-consciousness to these other realities?

Descartes begins by analyzing his own doubt. He knows he is doubting, because he cannot doubt that he is doubting without establishing doubt. To doubt doubt is to doubt. For Descartes to know that he is doubting, he has to know that he lacks certainty. This lack of certainty involves discerning the imperfect from the perfect. To discern this, he reasons, he first has to have a notion of perfection (at least with respect to certitude). This clear and distinct idea of perfection has to have a cause. He also reasons that there cannot be more in the effect than there is in the cause. Only a perfect being can cause the idea of perfection. If the idea of perfection is real, its cause must also be real. Descartes concludes that God is the perfect cause of his idea of perfection. For

Descartes it is a short step from "I think, therefore I am" to "I think, therefore God is" *(Cogito, ergo Deus est)*.

Having reached the conviction that God is and is perfect, Descartes removes from his mind the doubtful notion that God is a great deceiver.

From the existence of himself and of God, Descartes proceeds to prove the existence of the external world. He seeks to prove this with the idea of *extension*. While the idea of God's nonexistence is absurd (to conceive of a perfect being one must conceive of it as being, not as nonbeing), the idea of extension is *not* contradicted by conceiving of non-existing extension. That the mind can conceive of extension in geometrical forms does not prove that such forms exist in reality. In addition to the notion of extension, we also have sensations, including the sensation that we have physical bodies. We have an overwhelming inclination to believe that the sensations we experience come from bodies (extended) other than our own. Either this inclination comes from God or God is a deceiver. But God is not a deceiver; therefore the sensations we experience and our notion of extension must come to us from an external world.

Thought and Matter

A major problem Descartes seeks to solve is the relationship between thought and matter. The physical realm is the realm of extension. Matter must be extended; it must take up space. Thought, on the other hand, is not extended; ideas do not take up space and they have no weight (even ideas deemed to be "weighty").

Descartes faces the question of how thought and action are related. What is the relationship between mind and body? For example, to complete this sentence I must decide to push my pen along the paper. Writing is a physical action. I have the idea in my mind of what words to write, and from this idea flows the act of writing. I am moving from the mental to the physical. A moment ago my thoughts were interrupted because I experienced a pain in one of the fingers holding my pen. I have been writing all morning, and the pain in my finger provoked me to interrupt my chain of thought and consider taking a break. In this case the process of thought and action, matter and mind, was reversed. The action or material sensation in my finger gave rise to a thought.

How does this work? How does thought produce action and action produce thought when one of them (thought) is nonextended and nonmaterial while the other (action) is extended and material?

Descartes' approach to this problem is ingenious. Falling back on his knowledge of math, he argues that the transition between thought and action, or what he calls "interaction," takes place in a *point* in the pineal gland in the brain. In mathematics a point takes up space but has no definite extended length. Presumably a line can have an infinite number of points on it. The "point" is neither fish nor fowl, being neither extended *nor* nonextended, and therefore it can serve as the transition between the two.

In the case of his theory of interaction, Descartes does not achieve clear and distinct conclusions according to his own rules. He is left with a nagging dualism between mind and body. His speculation concerning the relationship of extension and nonextension, however, laid the foundation for crucial issues of causality that would be probed by his disciples and other philosophers.

Two of Descartes' followers devised theories of the mind and body called *occasionalism*. One of them, Arnold Geulincx, denies all causal interaction between mind and body. Mind and body are two separate and distinct substances that cannot directly cause each other to do anything. Geulincx admits that when a person decides to move his arm, his arm actually moves. But, he says, the mind or the will is not the cause of the arm's moving. The primary cause of all actions is God. When my mind thinks about moving my arm, God creates or causes the movement. This theory deems the causality between mind and body to be secondary. The two operate in a parallel way due to the primary causality of God.

7

John Locke:
Father of Modern Empiricism

The rationalism that dominated the seventeenth century was not limited to the Cartesian school. Jewish philosopher Baruch Spinoza built on the work of René Descartes but took rationalism in a new direction. Spinoza was a mathematician (like Descartes) who specialized in geometry, and he constructed a philosophy based on axioms that can be used to explain reality.

The question of the relationship between thought and action, which Descartes sought to explain with his theory of interactionism, poses a major theological question: How is God related to the world, particularly with respect to causality? As science made progress in its attempt to explain the "laws" of nature, the idea became increasingly popular that nature operates much like a machine, which runs according to its built-in parts.

This provoked a crisis with respect to the Judaeo-Christian view of divine providence, which sees God as not only the creator of the universe but also its governor. Historically, the laws of nature had been seen as the law of God. All things live and move and have their being in him. According to the classic view, all power in this world is derived from the power of God, meaning that the universe does not and cannot function independently from God. The universe is equally dependent on God's power for its origin and for its continued existence.

With respect to causality, Christian philosophies of the seventeenth century distinguished between *primary* and *secondary* causality. God alone is the primary cause of all things, but he works in and through secondary causes. Secondary causes are real causes, but they depend ultimately on God for their potency.

For example, when it rains the grass gets wet. Customarily we assign the causal power for this to the rain. Wet grass is the effect or result of the causal power of the rain's falling upon it. What role does God have in the process? The traditional answer was that the grass gets wet ultimately due to the providence of God, who ensures that rain falls to make the grass wet. Without this primary cause, there could be no secondary cause (the rain) to do the job.

This theistic view of the world precludes the notion that the universe operates in a mechanistic fashion under its own power. The tension between a theistic universe governed by God and a mechanistic universe closed to divine interference from God was a burning issue at this time, evidenced by the Cartesian occasionalists who sought to ground nature's dependence and its "laws" in the activity of God.

Substance Philosophy

Spinoza takes a different approach to the question in his "substance philosophy." His famous maxim, *Deus sive natura* ("God or nature"), which identifies God with the whole of nature, gave rise to the view that Spinoza advocated a form of pantheism. In simple or crass terms, pantheism means that all is God or that God is all. The fundamental problem with this definition is that it renders the term *God* meaningless. If God is everything in general, then he is nothing in particular. If he cannot be individuated, then there is no need or it makes no sense to assign to the word *God* any meaning.

Spinoza, however, is not simplistic. Though he does not distinguish between God and the world absolutely, he does distinguish between two aspects of nature. He defines God as *substance*. This substance is self-existent. Substance has an infinite number of attributes. An attribute is a particular manifestation of substance; it is that which the mind perceives. All things are contained in God and substance, but substance differs in its aspects.

Spinoza distinguishes between *natura naturans* and *natura naturata*. What is the difference? The *natura naturans* refers to God's substance and attributes by which he acts. The *natura naturata* are the modes of God's attributes or the ways in which God expresses or manifests himself in the world.

For Spinoza, an attribute is a particular manifestation of substance and a mode is a particular manifestation of an attribute. All the modes in which thought and action take place in this world, however, are ultimately determined by God's substance. All modes of reality are fixed from eternity. Thought and action may be distinguished, but they may not be separated. Their "interaction" is rooted in substance. All that happens, happens by necessity.

Preestablished Harmony

Gottfried Wilhelm Leibniz, born in 1646, was also an accomplished mathematician. He is credited with developing calculus before Isaac Newton, though Newton claimed to be first. Leibniz developed a complex cosmology based on what he calls "monads," the elemental atoms of reality.

With respect to the vexing problem of the relationship between thought and action, we look to Leibniz's theory of *preestablished harmony*. Each individual unit of reality, or monad, acts according to its peculiar, created purpose. Though each monad exists in virtual isolation from every other monad, monads act together in symphonic harmony. Events cannot be sufficiently explained by

looking simply at their proximate or immediate causes; the immediate cause of something does not adequately explain the whole.
An immediate cause may be an *efficient* reason for an effect, but
it is not a *sufficient* reason for it. The sufficient reason is not proximate but remote. (Leibniz was searching for an explanation of
the appearance of design in the universe, an explanation of why the
cosmos displays order rather than chaos.)

If we had only an astronomical number of particular causes
for particular things, said Leibniz, we might be able to explain a
cause for a simple action or event, but we could not explain how
all of the causes fit together. This is the ancient question of the
one and the many, unity and diversity. A plural number of particular causes could yield a multiverse but never a universe. To discover a sufficient reason for the whole, one must look outside of
or beyond the series of particular causes to a transcendent cause.
Only a transcendent or "primary" cause provides a sufficient
reason for what may be deemed secondary causes.

Because all monads and their interrelatedness are orchestrated
ultimately by God, Leibniz can argue that we live in the best of
all possible worlds. It is usually granted that Leibniz was the
model for Voltaire's Dr. Pangloss.[1]

Unlocking Locke

If Descartes may be considered the father of modern rationalism,
then the title "father of modern empiricism" may be given to John
Locke (though some grant it to Francis Bacon). Locke (1632–1704)
lived most of his life in the seventeenth century, but his influence was
felt mostly in the eighteenth century, commonly called the age of
British empiricism.

Locke challenged rationalism at the point of its insistence on
innate ideas, or *a priori* knowledge. Locke's chief and most

famous work on this subject is *An Essay Concerning Human Understanding,* which appeared in 1690.[2]

Locke set out to inquire into the basic questions of epistemology. He sought to explore *how* human knowledge is acquired, and like Descartes he also wanted to discover *what* we can know. To answer the second question, he had to begin with the first: *How* we arrive at knowledge determines *what* we can know.

Just as Descartes is famous for his maxim *Cogito, ergo sum,* so Locke is known for his *tabula rasa,* the "blank tablet." Locke's first step is to challenge the rationalist ideal of clear and distinct innate ideas. He casts doubt on innate ideas by questioning their universality. He argues that not everyone knows such things as the laws of noncontradiction and causality. Children and the feeble-minded, for example, do not know these laws (a thesis refuted by Immanuel Kant, among others). Locke grants, however, that there is a "universal readiness" to assent to such principles (an admission that only serves to strengthen his critics).

According to Locke, a human person at birth has no innate ideas. The newborn's mind is a blank tablet. Nothing is already written on the pages of his mind. All knowledge, including the law of noncontradiction, is learned through experience. All knowledge is therefore *a posteriori.* (*A posteriori* knowledge comes after or "post" experience; *a priori* knowledge comes before or "prior" to experience.)

Locke argues that knowledge begins with simple *ideas.* These simple ideas are the raw material or building blocks of all knowledge. He defines an idea as whatever is in the mind. These simple ideas come from one of two sources, *sensation* and *reflection,* and sensation is the greater source.

The five senses are sight (visual), hearing (auditory), touch (tactile), smell (olfactory), and taste. Through the *sensations* expe-

rienced by our sensory organs, we become aware of ideas such as
white and blue, hot and cold, bitter and sweet, hard and soft,
and fragrant and malodorous. That which the five senses perceive is called "empirical" reality.

Reflection involves awareness, thinking, doubting, reasoning, willing, and other activities of the mind.

All ideas can be traced back to either sensation or reflection.
And all ideas are either simple or complex.

A simple idea is unmixed and uniform. It cannot be broken
down into parts. The music of Johann Sebastian Bach, for example,
can be broken down into discrete individual notes—the notes themselves are simple, but their arrangement into a cantata is complex.

Locke identifies four kinds of simple ideas. The first is the
discrete sensory data we have described. The second is discrete
reflections. The third is qualities discovered through the co-operation of the senses (I see a steak on the grill; at the same time I
smell its aroma and hear it sizzle). The fourth kind is ideas derived
from a co-operation of sense and reflection.

Complex Ideas

Complex ideas, Locke explains, derive from the raw data of simple ideas. To receive simple ideas the mind may be relatively passive. It is like a tablet someone writes on. The tablet does not
create the words but merely receives them. To move from simple
ideas to complex ideas the mind must be active, functioning more
like a computer than a simple tablet. The mind undertakes the
basic activities of *combining, comparing,* and *separating,* sometimes called *compounding, abstracting*, and *relating*, respectively.
In this process the mind joins ideas together and individuates
and separates them.

For example, the simple idea of space comes from recognizing the distance between two bodies. From repeated, single experiences of space we build up the complex idea of immense space. From a similar experience of seconds we construct the complex idea of eternity, even though we have never experienced eternity as such. Though the idea of eternity is *a priori* (that is, prior to the experience of eternity), it is nevertheless *a posteriori* because it has been built on a prior experience of moments of time.

Of course one must ask if the idea of space or time is ever really a "simple" idea. We gain an idea of space, for example, only by relating the simple sensations of two objects. (This question will be raised later by David Hume.)

Locke must explain the formation of complex ideas in order to explain the phenomenon of language itself.

Here we face once more the ancient question of universals. Locke contends that universals do not have real being, arguing that only individuals exist. Yet he is reluctant to say (with the nominalists) that universals are merely names generated by the mind. He acknowledges that the mind does "create" universals, but he concludes (with metaphysical skeptics) that we cannot know the real essences of things.

Locke embraces the "correspondence" theory of truth, which eschews pure subjectivism or relativism. He defines truth as "that which corresponds to reality." This is what Francis Schaeffer calls "true truth." When he uses this phrase, Schaeffer is not stuttering or indulging in redundancy, but is speaking of truth that is objective and not dependent merely on the believing subject.

Locke's problem with objective truth comes at the point of one's getting in touch with reality. He faces the ancient subject-object problem: Objective truth must be subjectively appropriated. How can I know for sure that reality is as it appears to me? The bridge between my mind and the world outside of me is my five senses. Can I rely on sense perception to get to the objective world? Locke is aware of this subject-object problem and tackles it by distinguishing between primary and secondary qualities.

Primary and Secondary Qualities

Since Locke acknowledges that we have no direct perception of essences, he must explain how we get in touch with reality. According to Locke, we get in touch with reality by perceiving the *qualities* of objects. He distinguishes between *primary qualities* and *secondary qualities*. Primary qualities inhere in the bodies themselves. When we are in touch with something's primary qualities, we are in touch with the thing itself. We do not perceive its essence, but by perceiving its primary qualities we do perceive its objective reality. These primary qualities are *inseparably related* to the thing itself, just as Aristotle's *accidens* were inseparably related to *substances*. A baseball looks round, for instance, because it *is* round. When a pitcher throws a baseball, it looks like it is moving because it *is* moving. Primary qualities refer to solidity (a baseball feels solid because it is solid), extension, figure, motion or rest, and number (when we see one baseball, we do so because it is not at the same time two baseballs).

Secondary qualities are those qualities that do not inhere in an object; rather, they are qualities that the object has the power to create *in us*. For example, we describe a baseball as white, but whiteness does not inhere in the ball. When we turn out the lights, the baseball has no color. Likewise we think a snowball is cold, but coldness does not inhere in the snowball. Rather, it merely feels cold to us relative to the temperature of our body. (Later studies indicate that coldness is merely the lack of heat.) When I put ice cubes in a glass of tea, the coldness of the cubes is not transferred to the tea. Instead, the cubes absorb the heat from the tea, reducing the tea's temperature. I get cold on a wintry day, not because the air chills me but because my body heat is lost trying to warm the surrounding air. For Locke, secondary qualities are such things as color, sound, taste, and odor. A thing may "stink" to me because it offends my olfactory sense, but the stink is not inherent in the object. One person finds the taste of broccoli pleasant, while another finds it repulsive. These are subjective reactions.

With respect to the substances that produce primary and secondary qualities, Locke assumes a commonsense view. He finds it necessary to assume the basic reliability of sense perception; we must assume that sensations are caused by something other than the projections of our minds. Substance is the cause of sensation. If there were no substantive realities, there could be no sensations. Locke falls back on the logic of Descartes in reasoning that there can be no thinking apart from something that thinks.

With respect to theism, Locke argues that the idea of God is not clear and distinct, nor is it innate. He does not reject the idea of God, however, but argues for God's existence empirically—not that we have an empirical sensation of God himself, but that his existence is a necessary inference gained from reflection. The idea of God, like the idea of substance, is inferred from other simple ideas. God is not subject to observation but is known by way of *demonstration.*

That God is known by demonstration does require the use of logic, which is intuitive. Locke grants this by intuitive knowledge, such as our sure knowledge that a square is not a circle. Intuitive knowledge assures us that a nonentity cannot produce real being. If this is so, then there has to have been something from eternity, or nothing would or could be now. Locke argues that knowledge of God's existence is more certain than anything our senses have not immediately revealed to us.

Political Philosophy

In America Locke is perhaps better known for his political theory than for his epistemology. His *Two Treatises of Civil Government*[3] has had a lasting impact on Great Britain and the United States. Locke says all law is grounded in natural law *(lex naturalis)*, and natural law in turn is rooted in the eternal law of God *(lex aeternitatis)*.

Locke differentiates three types of law: 1) the law of opinion, 2) civil law, and 3) divine law (see fig. 7.1). The law of opinion refers to general precepts established by public opinion. It is the "law of fashion," which may merely reflect what is in vogue or what is a group's collective preference. In modern parlance we may call this "contemporary community standards." This law may or may not be reflected in civil legislation, though it tends to be written into statutes sooner or later. It remains distinct from civil law, however, unless or until it is so enacted. The law of opinion is "enforced" by the court of public opinion with its moral sanctions, not by police or courts.

Civil law is enacted by governments and enforced by law-enforcement agencies. The virtue of civil law is measured against the standard of natural law, which in turn rests on the law of God. Language such as, "We are endowed by our Creator with certain inalienable rights . . ." is Lockean to the core. Locke asserts that the divine law, with its great principles of morality, can be discovered without reading the Bible; the divine law can be known through natural reason, because the divine law is known through natural law. He believes that the divine moral law is as demonstrable as the laws of mathematics.

Locke gives examples of such moral laws. First, where there is no property, there is no injustice. The idea of property involves a right to something. Injustice occurs when a human right is vio-

Figure 7.1
Sources of Civil Law

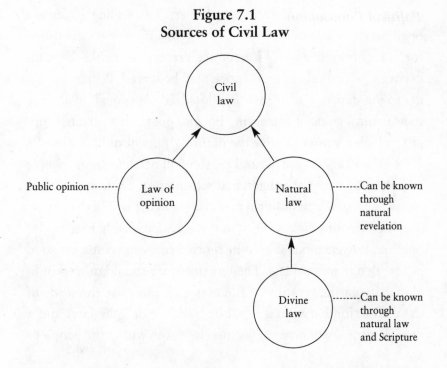

lated, as in the theft of private property. A second example is
that no government allows absolute liberty. No government exists
without some laws, and every law restricts somebody's liberty. For
example, a law against theft restricts the robber's freedom to steal
with impunity. This principle is analytically true.

Private property rights, according to Locke, precede civil law
because they are grounded in natural law. It is necessary to restrict
the freedom of some people (such as the thief) because in the
state of nature evil is present. In a state of nature without civil government, the "law of the people," where might makes right, pre-
vails. To protect humans from other humans, government is
necessary. As Augustine maintains, government is not so much a
necessary evil as a necessity because of evil.

People in a community agree to limit some of their freedoms

in order to have an orderly and just society. This willing agreement or *social contract* establishes the state. Government is established for the common good. Courts are created to settle disputes between individuals so that justice may be served. People surrender to the state not *all* of their freedom but just enough to achieve their natural goals of preserving life and possessing private property, which together involve the natural "pursuit of happiness."

Locke believes that natural reason will persuade most people to pursue a course of enlightened self-interest. He favors a commonwealth in which political power rests in the will of the majority. The laws of a just state should not reside merely in majority opinion, however, but should be motivated by the common good as revealed in natural law. The law of nature should protect individuals from the tyranny of the majority. Here are the seeds of the distinction between a republic (where rule is by law) and a pure democracy (where rule is merely by the will of the people).

David Hume:
Skeptic

Between the work of John Locke and the devastating skepticism of David Hume stood the fascinating figure of George Berkeley. Though also a student of mathematics and logic, Berkeley's chief concerns were the fields of philosophy and theology. Born in Ireland in 1685, he enrolled in Trinity College, Dublin, in 1700. Ordained in the Church of England, he was made a bishop in 1734. He spent three years in America, during which he probably had frequent encounters with the American philosophical genius Jonathan Edwards.

Berkeley is best known for his controversial maxim *Esse est percipi,* "To be is to be perceived," a maxim that has provoked endless attempts at humor. Though a carefully conceived epistemological formula, it has prompted such questions as, "If a tree falls in the forest and no one is there to hear it, does it make a sound?" Or its more modern, "politically correct" version: "If a man says something and a woman is not there to hear him, is he still wrong?"

The motto *Esse est percipi* seeks to summarize the essence of Berkeley's insight. He begins his analysis of human knowledge by arguing that whatever may or may not really exist outside of us, we can know only what is actually imprinted on our senses or can be remembered of our sensations, and what we can know by reflecting on ideas. All we can ever know, then, is ideas. He takes an ax to the root of the tree of the knowledge of metaphys-

Table 8.1
Maxims of Modern Philosophers

Cogito, ergo sum.	I think, therefore I am.	René Descartes
Deus sive natura	God or nature	Baruch Spinoza
Tabula rasa	A blank tablet (referring to the mind at birth)	John Locke
Esse est percipe.	To be is to be perceived.	George Berkeley

ical essences or things in themselves. In a certain sense Berkeley considers Locke's distinction between primary and secondary qualities to be arbitrary. For Berkeley all qualities are secondary in that nothing exists unless it is perceived.

But Berkeley's theory is no simplistic retreat into subjectivism. He denies, not that objective reality exists, but that objective reality can exist apart from its being perceived. He distinguishes between the activity of the mind *(percipere)* and the impression received by the mind *(percipi),* between the products of an active imagination, which are a matter of willful fabrication, and passively received sense impressions, which occur apart from one's volition.

Before going to bed last night, I fed the fish in the pond outside my house. When I awoke this morning, I went outside and fed the fish again. Did my fish and pond continue to exist while I was sleeping and not perceiving them? We may *assume* they remained in existence during the night because they were there again in the morning, but they were not "there" all night in my mind because I was not perceiving them. My *idea* of the pond and the fish was there last night, and my idea of them was there again this morning. On both occasions my perception of them was passive and involuntary. I did not conjure them up by imaginative whim. To account for the continuity of the fish and the pond, other philosophers have posited an abstract concept of material substance, an external reality I can never perceive.

The question of regularity in the sequence of ideas or perceptions leads people to assume that there is an ongoing, material substratum to external reality and that physical, mechanistic causes are involved in the interplay between physical things.

For example, science "explains" that tides are caused by the gravitational pull or "attraction" of the moon and that dropped objects fall to the ground because of gravitational attraction, a force that, in itself, cannot be perceived. Scientists formulate this mysterious attraction as follows: Two particles of matter attract each other as the product of their masses and inversely as the square of the difference.

A question has been raised about this mysterious force of attraction by twentieth-century Christian philosopher Gordon Clark: Does the concept of "attraction" really enlarge our knowledge? Does one atom put on lipstick and deodorant and have its hair styled in order to "attract" another atom? Is the term *attraction* merely a subterfuge to conceal our ignorance? Do we infuse the concept of "attraction" with ontological power or being, much as we do the concept of "chance"?

When reading the theories of eighteenth-century thinkers, we frequently encounter references to "animal spirits" that carry impulses in our nervous systems. These casual references to animal spirits amuse us, striking us as naïve and nonsensical concepts. But are they any more nonsensical than our modern terms, which are equally unperceived?

Describing an event, a process, or a motion does not necessarily explain it. Even if our descriptions come in the form of mathematical equations that yield a certain predictability, does that mean we have achieved *knowledge* of reality? Like Ptolemy's geocentric system, our theories can "save the phenomena" without achieving accurate knowledge of reality.

Take, for example, the nature of energy. We ask, "What *is*

energy?" One may reply, "It is the ability to do work." But we push harder and say, "We are asking, not what energy can *do*, but what it *is*." One may then reply, "$E=MC^2$." But we become obstreperous and say, "We are asking not for energy's mathematical equivalent, but about its nature. What is the difference between energy and boojums? Between energy and animal spirits? Between energy and attraction?" We do not directly perceive energy, yet it is an unassailable doctrine of modern empirical science.

This is not to say that the existence of such a thing as energy is a mere gratuitous assumption. It is, however, a theory to explain unknown actions. If matter itself, in itself, cannot be perceived, how can its corollary, energy, which also cannot be perceived in its essence, be any better known?

Here Berkeley turned to God as the ultimate cause of involuntary ideas. He calls in God to account for the intersubjective objectivity of the real world. God becomes the indispensable perceiver whose ideas provide the basis of all reality.

At this point we see a modification in the correspondence theory of truth (i.e., truth is that which corresponds to reality). Berkeley amended this definition to read: Truth is that which corresponds to reality as it is perceived by God. God is the great perceiver by and in whose ideas reality exists. My pond and fish continue to exist while I sleep because they are continuously being perceived by God. (This laid the groundwork for the curious theological concept of "continual creation.")

David Hume

It has often been said that in the work of David Hume we enter the "graveyard" of British empiricism. He took the empirical approach to the depths of skepticism. Many believe that Hume destroyed once and for all the law of causality, and that in so doing he opened the door to the idea that anything can produce anything (a statement that, as we will see, still relies on the law of causality for "production"). But before considering Hume's famous critique of causality, we must first look at his epistemology.

Born in Edinburgh, Scotland, in 1711, Hume spent many years in France and elsewhere on the Continent, numbering among his friends Jean-Jacques Rousseau and Adam Smith. In 1739 he published *A Treatise of Human Nature*,[1] which was a literary flop. After the success of *Essays Moral and Political*,[2] however, he revised his first book and retitled it *An Enquiry Concerning Human Understanding*,[3] which is now considered a philosophical classic. He wrote other important works, including the posthumously published *Dialogue Concerning Natural Religion*.[4] He died a wealthy man in Edinburgh in 1776.

In analyzing epistemology, Hume argues that the total content of the mind can be reduced to the data provided by sensory experience, or *perceptions*. These perceptions take two forms, *impressions* and *ideas*. The original data are the impressions; copies or memories of the impressions are ideas. What the mind remembers (ideas) is directly related to the *intensity* or *vivacity* of the original impressions—to their degree of "liveliness."

This point is noted by memory experts, who seek to get the original impressions in mind by the most graphic devices possible. Memory experts will transform numbers into (sometimes bizarre) pictures to render them more vivid and less abstract. Any student of foreign languages knows it is easier to memorize nouns than verbs, and verbs than prepositions or conjunctions, because nouns are more concrete and vivid than verbs, and verbs communicate more intense action than prepositions. (Some argue that this notion of vivacity and intensity was self-consciously employed by Jonathan Edwards in his sermons, to make a "lasting impression.")

For Hume there can be no ideas without impressions. At the

point of origin, all ideas are based on simple impressions. Not all impressions, however, originate in sensations. Some impressions are gained from *reflection upon* sensations. We often have desires, emotions, and passions that follow ideas on which we have reflected.

The faculty that enables us to construct complex ideas out of simple ideas and impressions is the *imagination*. The imagination assembles and reassembles the discrete units of sensation. Hume argues that whatever is *distinct* is therefore *distinguishable,* and whatever is distinguishable is by thought or imagination *separable*. All of our perceptions are, insofar as we have them, *distinct*. If distinct, they must also be *distinguishable*. For instance, the mind notices the difference between a tree and a butterfly. They may thus be conceived of as existing *separately* and may actually exist separately without contradiction.

Wherever ideas have distinct qualities, the ideas may be associated with each other by the imagination. These qualities include 1) resemblance, 2) contiguity in time and space, and 3) cause and effect. A picture, for instance, leads our thoughts to the original through resemblance; one room in a house introduces inquiry about other rooms in the house (contiguity); and the memory of a wound produces reflection on the pain that resulted from the wound (cause and effect). Ideas are associated in these three ways, but according to Hume the most central building block of knowledge is the notion of cause and effect. This is the foundation on which the validity of all knowledge depends. If the causal principle is flawed, there can be no certain knowledge.

The Law of Causality

Hume begins his inquiry into causality by exploring the origin of the very idea of causality. He points out that, in the theories of causality propounded by the Cartesian occasionalists and by Baruch Spinoza, Gottfried Wilhelm Leibniz, John Locke, and George Berkeley, there was no agreement on the actual cause of a given event or action. Was the action a result of direct interaction between thought and extension? Was it an occasion for God to act? Was it through substance and its attributes and modes? Was it through preestablished harmony? Was it through the continuous perception of God?

Hume begins his own analysis by noting that the idea of cause and effect arises from reflection on certain relationships between objects. The law of causality says that A causes B. But how do we *know* that A causes B? Empirical experience furnishes three reasons for speaking of causal relationships. First, A and B always occur close together spatially *(contiguity)*. Second, the cause always precedes the effect *(priority with respect to time)*. And third, we always see A followed by B *(constant conjunction)*. Together these elements create a commonsense assumption that there is some sort of *necessary connection* between A and B. Hume challenges this assumption.

The assumption of causality, says Hume, rests first of all on customary relationships. For example, we have repeated experiences of rain followed by wet grass. First, the two are *contiguous,* appearing close together spatially; if rain falls over my front yard, my front yard is the place that gets wet. Second, my lawn gets wet after it rains, not before it rains *(priority with respect to time)*. Third, every time it rains over my yard (A), my grass gets wet (B). This phenomenon indicates a customary relationship *(constant conjunction)* between the rain and my wet grass, which I assume is some kind of necessary connection.

Hume uses an illustration from pocket billiards, which I will summarize. If I desire to sink the 9-ball in the corner pocket, I pick up the cue stick and rub some chalk on the tip, then I aim at the cue ball to direct its path to strike the object ball (the 9-ball) so as to impart to it motion that will send it merrily on its way to the designated pocket. This process involves several actions. For the cue stick to strike the cue ball, I must set the stick in motion with my arm. I move the stick to strike the cue ball while the cue ball is stationary. The cue ball then moves across the table and collides with the 9-ball. Now the 9-ball moves toward the corner pocket (if my aim and stroke have been accurate). It looks something like figure 8.1.

In this process I assume that my arm's motion causes the cue stick to move, the cue stick's motion causes the cue ball to move, the cue ball's motion causes the object ball to move, and the motion of the object ball causes it to drop into the corner pocket.

I assume a causal relationship because of the *contiguous* relationship between these objects, the *temporal priority* of one action before another, and the *constant conjunction* of these actions that I know from repetition. But how do I know for sure that in making this assumption I am not violating the classic informal fallacy of logic called the *post hoc, ergo propter hoc* ("after this, therefore because of this") fallacy? When the rooster crows or the turkey gobbles just before the sun rises, has the rooster or turkey *caused* the sun to rise? If all roosters and turkeys were to become extinct, would the sun no longer rise?

The fact that the wrong cause may be assigned to an effect does not, however, mean that all causes are therefore "wrong." Hume does not prove that *nothing* causes the grass to get wet or the pool ball to move. Indeed, he could not prove such a thing. The law of causality is merely an abstract projection of the law of noncontradiction (that something cannot *be* what it is and *not be* what it is at the same time and in the same sense or relationship). To refute the law of causality one must refute the law of noncontradiction. But as Augustine demonstrated, to refute the

Figure 8.1
Hume's Illustration from Pocket Billiards

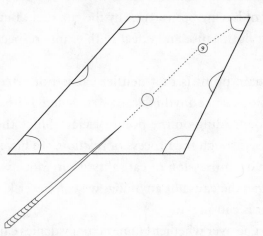

law of noncontradiction rationally, one must assume the law of noncontradiction to be valid.

We remember that the law of causality simply declares that every effect must have an antecedent cause. This law is analytically true and irrefutable—it is true by definition. An effect is, by definition, something that is caused, just as a cause is, by definition, something that yields an effect. Of course this does not in itself prove that there is such a thing as causality. For example, if we lived in a world where there were no effects, then there would also be no causes. Or, if we lived in a world where there were no causes, then there would be no effects. But if we live in a world where there *are* effects, then there must also be causes. The only world in which there are no effects and no causes would be a world in which everything is self-existent. Again, this does not mean that everything or anything in the world would be self-caused. Remember that something cannot be its own cause, or be a cause and effect at the same time and in the same relation. Indeed, something could be both a cause and an effect at the

same time, but not in the same relationship. The cue ball could
be at the same time the *cause* of the movement of the object ball
and the *effect* of having been struck by the cue stick. But here the
cue ball is not both cause and effect in the same respect or relationship.

Hume's main point is that neither cause nor effect can be
objective qualities, since anything can be considered either a cause
or an effect, depending on the point of view. Since the idea of
causality arises through the process of *relation,* we have no original sensation or impression of causality itself. Since we cannot
directly *perceive* the cause of anything, we can never know with
certainty what is causing it.

Experts argue over whether Hume actually denies causality or
is content to show that we cannot know that A causes B—that
no object implies the existence of another when we consider
objects individually. Hume may be correct with respect to the
idea of objects. But the idea of cause itself necessarily implies the
idea of effect, and vice versa. This again is a *formal* truth.

When Hume, in his skepticism, declares that anything can
produce anything, we have to ask what he means by the term
produce? Is this not merely another word for cause? It is important that Hume rules out chance as a possible cause for anything,
understanding that the word *chance* is a substitute for the word
ignorance.

Hume's skepticism goes beyond the realm of pure causality
to the ideas of the self, substance, and God, because none of these
can be discovered by an original sensation or impression. Hume
denies that we have any idea of the self, which is like saying I
have no idea of I. But it's not that simple. Here he speaks in terms
of an original idea based on impression or sensation. In a word,
the self cannot be known empirically. This skepticism was fodder
for Immanuel Kant.

The Possibility of Miracles

Hume understands that the concept of *miracle* is crucial to the Judaeo-Christian faith. Take away miracles and you take away Christianity. Earlier Locke had said that biblical miracles certify the "credit of the proposer." That is, miracles do not prove the existence of God (his existence must be established before a work can be credited to him), but they demonstrate God's certification of an agent of revelation. Moses was given miraculous powers in order to prove that his message was from God. Likewise, Jesus' truth claims were demonstrated by his miracles, and especially his miraculous resurrection from the dead.

Hume defines a miracle as a violation of natural law. Natural law is established by repetitive, uniform experience. For an event to be deemed a miracle, it must go against or depart from the uniform experience of nature. The uniform experience establishes the law. No one has ever experienced a miracle, because no one can have an experience that violates the pattern of uniformity. Hume sinks into the slough of circular reasoning, violating the *petitio principi* principle of logic. He rules out the very possibility of a miracle at the beginning.

How does he do this? Hume speaks of "probability quotients" of natural experience. If 100,000 squirrels are found with bushy tails, what happens when someone claims to have discovered a squirrel with a patent-leather tail? The claim represents a radical departure from the norm. The odds against such a squirrel in this case are 100,000 to 1, an extremely small probability quotient. In fact, the probability quotient against a miracle will always be higher than the probability for it. In addition, a claim to a unique event has no credibility when placed against the uniformity of experience.

For example, a popular Christian argument for the Resurrection is that Jesus' disciples must have been telling the truth concerning his resurrection because they were willing to die for this conviction. From one perspective the disciples' willingness to die for their belief certainly adds a degree of credibility to their claim. But is it decisive? "Which is more likely," Hume would ask, "that deluded fanatics would die for their delusion or that a man would come back to life from the dead?" The answer is obvious. All things being equal, it is more likely that men will die for a delusion than that one of them (or anyone else) would come out of the grave alive.

The case for the resurrection of Christ, however, involves far more than the likelihood of fanatics dying for delusions. It entails the consideration of 1) God's existence and nature, 2) the relationship of death to sin, 3) the sinlessness of Christ, 4) predictive prophecy centuries before the event, 5) the testimonies of multiple witnesses, 6) the credibility of those witnesses, and so forth.

How interesting that what Hume deems impossible, the biblical writers deem necessary. Given the character of Jesus, the New Testament argues that it was impossible for death to hold him.

If Hume were to apply his criticism of miracle consistently, he would rule out not only miracle but all empirical evidence. There can be no "uniform empirical experience" without repetition. To have a "uniform experience" of grass getting wet when it rains, there must be a first occurrence. For something to be repeated, it must occur at least twice. Manifestly, for something to occur twice, it must occur once. But when something occurs the first time, it is a unique event. As an event out of the bounds of uniform experience, its occurrence must be denied. If the first occurrence is denied, there cannot be a second. The "second" would be a "first," and it would be eliminated just as the first "first" was.

Thus it is never possible to get to the point of repetition. By Hume's reasoning, there can be no beginning to the world, no "big bang," nothing unique.

Hume's legacy was a skepticism with respect not merely to God and religion but also to science. This skepticism awakened Immanuel Kant from his dogmatic slumber.

Immanuel Kant: Revolutionary Philosopher

The thought of Immanuel Kant represents the watershed of modern philosophy. The impasse between rationalism and empiricism had created a crisis of skepticism. Kant's new synthesis of epistemology was no less significant than Plato's much earlier synthesis of Heraclitus and Parmenides.

The philosophical revolution created by Kant may have had a greater impact than the Copernican revolution in science and more far-reaching consequences than the American Revolution in politics. Ironically the Kantian revolution was taking place at the same time in history as the American Revolution. Kant's most famous work, *Critique of Pure Reason,* was published in 1781.[1]

Kant is important not only for creating a new synthesis of rationalism and empiricism but also for destroying the classical synthesis Thomas Aquinas had achieved in his natural theology. Many assume that Kant destroyed the traditional arguments for God's existence once and for all, saying that Kant eliminated reason and made room for faith.

Kant was the product of a strange mixture: He received early training in Pietism (a German religious movement spearheaded by Philipp Spener), and he was influenced by the Enlightenment, especially Jean-Jacques Rousseau.

The Enlightenment *(Aufklärung),* which swept Europe (particularly Germany, France, and England) in the eighteenth century, was not a monolithic movement. In the sphere of epistemology it spawned what is called the analytical method of knowing, which forms the heart of the scientific method. The analytical method, which is not unlike Aristotle's, combines the elements of induction and deduction, seeking "the logic of the facts." One gathers the facts inductively and empirically, then searches for the pattern of universal laws operating within the facts. This method was employed, for example, in the political philosophy of Montesquieu and the economic theory of Adam Smith.

Some Enlightenment thinkers, such as Christian Wolff, whose textbooks Kant devoured, were friendly toward theism, but many others were openly hostile. Most hostile to God were the French Encyclopedists, particularly Denis Diderot and Paul H. D. de Holbach, who declared himself the "personal enemy of God." These men concluded that the "God-hypothesis" is no longer necessary to account for the facts of the universe and human life. The phenomena can be "saved" without resorting to God. The origin of the universe can be explained without recourse to creation. The new theory that captured many of these thinkers was "spontaneous generation," which has since been widely, though not universally, rejected.

An essay by a Nobel Prize-winning physicist, whose name I will not mention to protect the guilty, declares that one can no longer affirm spontaneous generation; the theory must be modified to what the author calls "gradual spontaneous generation." This is a recasting of the formula "space plus time plus chance" as the scientific explanation for the origin of the universe.[2] It is both unscientific and unnatural to say that the world popped into being by itself, being its own cause, writes the author. The universe cannot create itself spontaneously or quickly. It can only do so gradually. It takes time for something to come from nothing. Nothing cannot do the job overnight!

When the Hubble telescope was launched from Cape Kennedy, another highly respected physicist said that the telescope would verify that between 12 and 17 billion years ago the universe "exploded into being." If it exploded *into being,* what did it explode out of or from? Nonbeing?

Nevertheless, the Enlightenment concept of spontaneous generation made it "respectable" for scientists to be entirely liberated from any dependence on theology in answering the question of origins.

Likewise Gotthold Ephraim Lessing proposed what is commonly known as "Lessing's Ditch": The contingent events of history cannot provide a basis for knowledge of the transcendent, eternal realm. An unbridgeable chasm or ditch separates this world from the so-called metaphysical or theological realm. No bridge is wide enough to span this ditch. You simply cannot get there from here.

This is the milieu Kant entered, insisting that nothing could destroy his personal belief in God but also that a knowledge of God cannot be demonstrated by "pure reason" *(reine vernuft)* or science.

Born in Königsburg, East Prussia, in 1724, Kant spent his entire life there, dying in 1804. It is said that he never traveled more than 100 miles from home. He was a man of remarkable discipline. His neighbors said they could set their watches by his daily walks, which began precisely at 4:30 P.M. Kant was consumed by two problems that seemed to defy explanation, "the starry heavens above and the moral law within." He was an avid student of Isaac Newton and wrote academic articles in the field of astronomy.

Enamored with the titanic progress of natural science, Kant

Table 9.1
Philosophers of the Enlightenment Era

	Birth–death	Place of birth	Primary place of residence	Philosopher and . . .	Position
Jean-Jacques Rousseau	1712–1778	Geneva	Paris	Litterateur	
Christian Wolff	1679–1754	Breslau, Poland	Halle and Marburg, Germany	Mathematician	Professor, Halle (1741–1754)
Denis Diderot	1713–1784	Langres, France	Paris	Encyclopedist	Editor, *Encyclopedie* (1751–1772)
Paul H. D. de Holbach	1723–1789	Edesheim, Germany	Paris	Encyclopedist	Baron
Gotthold Ephraim Lessing	1729–1781		Wolfenbütel, Germany	Dramatist, critic	Director, ducal library (1770–1781)

nevertheless argues that science cannot account for God or for human responsibility tied to moral freedom.

He is distressed by rationalism's dogmatism and its reluctance to incorporate empirical discoveries into its *a priori* and mathematical models. He is even more distressed with empiricism, because Hume's skepticism regarding causality makes scientific knowledge impossible. Kant also, with Newton, rules out chance as the genetic principle of this universe.

The Possibility of Knowledge

Kant employs in his critical philosophy the "transcendental method." In simple terms this means that to transcend certain problems of epistemology, one assumes that knowledge is not only needful but possible. Then Kant asks, "What is necessary for knowledge to take place?" or, "Under what conditions is knowledge possible?"

Kant's synthesis incorporates elements from both rationalism and empiricism. He agrees with empiricists that knowledge *begins* with experience, but he asserts that not all knowledge rises out of experience. For Kant there is also *a priori* knowledge. He agrees with Hume that we do not directly experience causality, yet he rejects the notion that causality is merely a psychological habit of connection. Our notion of causality, says Kant, comes from rational judgment, an operation of the faculty of the mind.

Knowledge begins, according to Kant, with the "sense manifold," which receives sensations and impressions. These sensations, however, are sorted out by categories built into the mind. Knowledge is a synergistic (co-operative) process between the senses and the mind. We have what Kant calls *pure intuitions of space and time*. No one can perceive either time or space. We cannot experience them in themselves. Yet every one of my perceptions I perceive in space and time. Without these *a priori* intuitions we could never have a discrete perception. For example, if I look out my window at this moment, I see trees, a pond, a waterfall, bushes, grass, and flowers, as well as blue sky and white, puffy clouds. I do not see a treespondwaterfallbushesgrassflowersskycloud. Without the pure intuitions of space and time, I could not individuate the data of experience or the words used to express them. I would have an indiscriminate, chaotic blurb of sensation that is unintelligible and meaningless.

It is the mind that provides unity to the diversity of my sensory experience. But it is not simply *the* mind; it is *my* mind. The subject that orders knowledge is the *self*. We know the self not through immediate sense perceptions (e.g., we cannot see it or hear it), but through what Kant calls the "transcendental unity of apperception" or the "transcendental apperception of the ego."

The self is apperceived, not perceived. It comes to me as a necessary implication of actual experience. We are immediately conscious of the self as a self. In this respect Kant is very close to
Descartes' primacy of self-consciousness.

The Limits of Knowledge

One of the most well-known elements of Kant's philosophy is his
distinction between the *phenomenal* and *noumenal* worlds (or
realms). Knowledge, according to Kant, is limited to the realm of
empirical experience. The sense manifold is the building block of
knowledge. The only realm we experience by sense perception is
the phenomenal world. As we have seen, *phenomena,* derived
from a Greek word meaning "manifest," refers to things that are
evident or manifest to the senses. We sometimes use the term
phenomenal to mean "fabulous, fantastic, exceedingly great," but
in philosophical jargon it refers to perceivable appearances. Thus
the phenomenal world is the world of appearances or the world as
we experience it with the senses.

Kant does not say that the phenomenal world is not real,
only that our knowledge is limited to it. When experiencing the
phenomena of this world, we do it *through* the lenses of our *a
priori* categories of thought. The objective world is perceived by
a thinking subject. This is not a case for solipsism or for the idea
that the external world is created by the subjective mind. Though
we can assume there are objects that exist in themselves, we can
never directly perceive the object itself without what is brought
to the experience by the mind.

The object or the thing-in-itself Kant calls the *Ding an sich*.
The *Ding an sich* really exists, but it exists in the *noumenal* realm,
beyond the reach of our senses. We cannot therefore know the
noumenal object or thing itself; we can know it only in a limited

fashion, as our senses perceive it in cooperation with the categories of our own mind. We never perceive the thing itself without the added categories of the mind.

As we have seen, the self also belongs to the noumenal realm, because we cannot perceive it directly, unaided by the mind. Neither the self nor the *Ding an sich* belongs to the phenomenal world. Since our knowledge is limited, first, to the phenomena and, second, by the manner in which our minds organize the raw data of experience, we cannot have "knowledge" of the self or of the *Ding an sich,* or at best our knowledge of these things is limited by these two factors.

Most important for Kant's role in the history of philosophy, he includes *God* in the noumenal realm. God, according to Kant, can never be perceived. He is not part of the sense manifold. The same limits that apply to our knowledge of things-in-themselves and our knowledge of the self apply to God. These are all part of the noumenal or metaphysical realm, about which knowledge is suspect. It is the phenomenal realm, not the noumenal realm, that is the arena of scientific inquiry.

The idea that God cannot be known by direct sense experience is not a novel idea in either philosophy or theology. The classic debate between natural theology and Kantian skepticism relates to the question of whether God can be known *mediately* through the phenomenal world. Thomas Aquinas, for example, insists that God (the noumenal) is known by and through the phenomenal. Aquinas argues this point from the New Testament, citing a passage from Paul: "What may be known of God is manifest in them, for God has shown it to them. For since the creation of the world His invisible attributes are clearly seen, being understood by the things that are made, even His eternal power and Godhead" (Rom. 1:19-20).

Paul argues that, although God is "invisible" or imperceivable, nevertheless he is "seen" and "known." Paul declares not that God is seen directly through sense perception but that he is perceived in and through the created order. For Paul the noumenal can be and is known through the phenomenal. If Kant is correct in his critique, then Paul is wrong. Conversely, if Paul is correct in his assertion, then Kant is wrong. Both cannot be right.

The Ontological Argument

The chief traditional arguments for God's existence are the ontological, cosmological, and teleological arguments. Kant gives close attention to the ontological argument as popularized by Anselm and later reformulated by Descartes and again by Wolff (with whom Kant was most familiar). According to Anselm, God is that being than which no greater can be conceived, and such a being must exist in reality as well as in the mind. Anselm's critic Gaunilo said that, just because he could conceive of a perfect island, this does not mean that such an island exists. Anselm replied that Gaunilo had missed the point. Anselm was not arguing (with conceptualism) that anything that can be rationally conceived by the mind must exist in reality. Rather, Anselm was limiting his argument to that being than which no greater can be conceived. If I conceive of a god who does not exist in reality, I am not thinking of Anselm's God, because a being who truly exists is greater than a mere mental construct.

Jonathan Edwards would later refine Anselm's argument by asserting that being cannot *not* be. Islands and dollars may not be, but being must be in order for it to be being. (This is more in line with Thomas's view of *necessary being*.)

Kant attacks the ontological argument on the grounds that *existence* is not a predicate—it is too elusive to receive formal definition. Existence is posited of a thing differently from its predicates (those things that can be affirmed or denied about it). One may know the fully determined essence of a thing, along with all its predicates, and still not know if it exists. Reason allows that such a God can or *may* exist in reality, but reason cannot know that God *does* exist.

Kant's rejection of the ontological argument fundamentally rests on his denial of existence as a predicate. In ordinary language, however, existence does function as a predicate. If we utter the word *God,* we are saying one thing. If we say, "God exists," we are saying something else, something that is not found merely in the word or idea *God* (Anselm to the contrary). But the issue remains: If existence is a predicate, is it something that must, by logical necessity, be attributed to God?

The Cosmological Argument

Kant argues against the cosmological argument for God's existence on the unusual grounds that, in the final analysis, it rests on the ontological argument. If the ontological argument is flawed, so is the cosmological argument.

Historically the cosmological argument has been the most popular and persistent argument for the existence of God. It is called "cosmological" because it reasons from the cosmos back to God as the cause of the cosmos. In short, the argument says that if anything exists, then an absolutely necessary being must also exist. It appeals to the law of causality: Since nothing can be its own cause, something must be uncaused or self-existent to account for the existence of anything.

The *ontological* argument moves from the idea of God to the reality of God, seeking to contain the argument within the limits of the formal arena of the mind, thereby avoiding the vagaries of sense perception or the empirical realm. The *cosmological* argument, on the other hand, begins usually with sense experience, a perception of things in the material world, or with self-consciousness.

A brief summary of the cosmological argument is in order. If we perceive that something (the self, the world, or anything in it) exists, then we are left with four options (some thinkers have sought other options, but these in turn can be reduced to one of the four, depending on how they are formulated):

1. The perceived "reality" is an illusion.
2. The reality is self-created.
3. The reality is self-existent.
4. The reality is ultimately caused or "created" by something that is self-existent.

Of these four options, two (options 3 and 4) include something that is self-existent. Option 2 is formally or logically impossible, for the notion of self-creation is analytically false. As we have seen, for something to create or cause itself, it must *be* before it is. It must be and not be, or exist and not exist, at the same time and in the same relationship. (A popular "fifth" option, an infinite regress or an infinite series of finite causes, may be reduced to option 2. It compounds the problem of self-creation infinitely.)

If option 2 is eliminated, the only rational alternative to something's being self-existent (necessary being) is option 1. If everything is an illusion, then nothing exists and we need not worry about knowing anything (there is nothing to know). But if all is an illusion, then the illusion itself is an illusion, which is self-defeating. If a perception or idea is illusory, then something or someone must be having the illusion. That is, there must be a cause for the illusion. The cause must be self-created, self-existent, or caused by something (ultimately created by something self-existent). So option 1 is resolved to options 3 or 4. We see then that the only two rationally possible options are 3 and 4, both of which have a self-existent something or necessary being.

All of this rests on the laws of noncontradiction and causality. Kant understands this and is unwilling to dispense with either reason or causality altogether. Instead he *limits the application of the law of causality*. He argues that the law of causality has no meaning or application except in the sensible world (that is, the world that can be perceived by the senses). This law applies to the phenomenal realm, not to the noumenal realm. It applies to the realm of physics, not metaphysics.

I have always been puzzled by Kant's insistence on this point. His limitation of causality to the phenomenal world seems arbitrary. If everything in the phenomenal world requires a cause, why does not the phenomenal world itself require a cause? I grant with David Hume that we have no immediate perception of causality, but our lack of perception of a particular cause does not allow us to conclude that there is no cause. We must keep in mind that the law of causality is a *formal* law, an extension of the law of noncontradiction.

At this point Kant links the cosmological argument to the ontological. If reason, formally considered, demands a necessary being (one that is both logically and ontologically necessary), this does not mean that a necessary being exists in reality. Because my reason tells me that logic demands a self-existent being, this does not mean that there is a self-existent being—unless reality is rational.

In defense of Thomas Aquinas and others who have reasoned cosmologically, I must say that they were proving "merely" that reason demands the existence of God. I do not know what else one could "reasonably" expect from reasoning other than that something is reasonable rather than unreasonable, rational rather than irrational. Again, if Kant remains skeptical about the application of causality to the metaphysical or noumenal world, why is he so san-

guine about its applicability to the phenomenal world? If one seeks
to be rational at one level, why not at both levels? Kant's limited
knowledge is a kind of limited skepticism that later philosophies
reject as a halfway house between full-orbed theism and nihilism.
To the nihilist, Kant was riding a roller coaster without brakes.

The Teleological Argument

Of the traditional proofs of God's existence, the teleological argument impressed both Hume and Kant the most. Kant grants that
the world is filled with things that display clear signs of orderliness
or purpose. It is difficult to conceive of design without a designer.
Some modern evolutionists have sought to account for design or
order with terms such as *chance* or *accidents*. It is troublesome
indeed to speak of "accidental purpose." This is similar to unintentional intentionality. This vexes Carl Sagan in his attempt to
describe the universe as cosmos rather than chaos; one cannot
have cosmos chaotically. Kant agrees that the pursuance of order
suggests an Orderer, but this brings one back to a dependence on
the law of causality as in the cosmological argument, and therefore results in the problems inherent in the ontological argument.

It is important to remember that Kant does not deny the existence of God. He does deny that God's existence can be rationally demonstrated, but he also denies that the idea of God can
be disproven rationally.

Kant's metaphysical and theological agnosticism is supported
by his theory of antinomies. Strictly speaking the word *antinomy* is, in historical parlance, a synonym for *contradiction*
(though it is now sometimes used loosely as a synonym for *paradox*). As the word *contradiction* derives from the Latin "to speak
against," the word *antinomy* derives from the Greek "against
law." The law against which an antinomy behaves is the law of

Table 9.2
Traditional Proofs of the Existence of God

	Beginning Point	Concise Summary
Ontological argument	Our idea of God	God is that being than which no greater being can be conceived. Such a being must exist in reality as well as in the mind.
Cosmological argument	Our sense experience of the cosmos	If anything exists, then an absolutely necessary being (God) must also exist.
Teleological argument	Empirical evidence of order and design	The world is filled with things that show signs of order and purpose. If the world is designed, then there must be a Designer (God).

noncontradiction. He lists several antinomies in philosophical reflection, including the following:

1. The world is limited in space and time, and the world is unlimited in space and time.
2. Every composite thing in the world is made up of simple parts, and no composite thing is made up of simple parts.
3. In addition to causality in the laws of nature, there is also freedom; and there is no freedom, since everything happens according to the laws of nature.
4. An absolutely necessary being exists as part of the world or as its cause, and no absolutely necessary being exists.

Kant is saying of these antinomies, not that both sets can be true, but that these counter-sets have been argued by metaphysicians and philosophers with equal force.

We must grant that philosophers have indeed argued forcibly for both sides of the antinomies. A forceful argument, however, is not necessarily a valid one. Let us consider antinomy 2. One can argue with great vigor that a composite thing is not made up of simple parts, but if it is not made up of parts (simple or complex), it is not composite. That a composite thing is made up of simple parts is analytically true (i.e., true by definition), and the most forceful argument in the world cannot falsify it. One can argue that there are no composite things in the world. But if there *are* composite things, they must consist of parts or they simply are not composite. People are quite capable of speaking nonsense, but they cannot speak nonsense intelligibly.

Although Kant notes the conclusions of different philosophers regarding these antinomies, he still holds that God is a useful *regulative idea*. A regulative idea, according to Kant, is one that is useful but not demonstrable, and for him such regulative ideas include not only the idea of God but also the idea of the self and of the *Ding an sich*.

Kant's Moral Argument for God

If in his criticism of the limits of theoretical thought Kant banishes God out the front door, he rushes to the back door to let God back in. In his moral and practical philosophy Kant seeks a basis for ethics. He argues for the presence of the "categorical imperative," a universal sense of oughtness that is integral to human experience and that provides a moral obligation or imperative to duty. Kant's version of the "Golden Rule" is this: "Act as if the maxim of thy action were to become a universal law of nature."

As Kant approaches epistemology in a transcendental way, so also he approaches ethics or moral philosophy. He asks the basic question, What would be necessary for ethics or the moral imperative to be meaningful? He concludes that for ethics to be meaningful there must be justice. Since justice does not work itself out perfectly in this world, there must be a future state in which justice will prevail. For justice to prevail, there must be a perfect Judge who is morally blameless, since a corrupt judge would not render perfect justice. This Judge must be omniscient, never erring in his judgment, and he must be omnipotent, ensuring that his justice is enacted.

In short, Kant argues for the Christian God on the basis that he must exist for ethics to be meaningful. Kant says that even if we cannot know that God exists, for practical purposes we must live "as if" he exists for ethics and society to be possible. He anticipates Fyodor Dostoyevsky's maxim, "If there is no God, all things are permissible." Without an absolute ethical norm, morality is reduced to mere preference and the world is a jungle where might makes right.

10

Karl Marx:
Utopian

Immanuel Kant's revolutionary philosophy was, as we have seen, a watershed in the history of theoretical thought. In one respect or another virtually all schools of philosophy that have developed since Kant have relied on him (see fig. 10.1).

Figure 10.1
Philosophies Arising from the Thought of Immanuel Kant

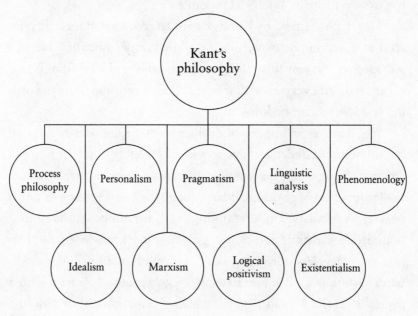

In the nineteenth century, due in large measure to Kant's metaphysical skepticism or agnosticism, philosophers turned their
attention to constructing a philosophy of history. Prior to Kant
the chief foci in philosophy were metaphysics and epistemology.
Since Kant they have been history and anthropology. This is not
to say that no one prior to Kant addressed these areas, or that
metaphysics and epistemology were completely abandoned after
Kant. Not every metaphysician rolled over and played dead at
Kant's feet. But the emphasis since Kant has clearly been in the area
of the phenomenal—the arena of this world. Since his day the
Western world has been waiting for a new Plato or Aristotle to
rescue metaphysics from a burgeoning skepticism.

In this brief overview of the history of philosophy, I nearly
decided to include a whole chapter on G. W. F. Hegel (1770–1831),
whose thought dominated at least the first half of the nineteenth
century. He is one of the most complex and difficult philosophers,
however, so perhaps the intimidation factor is what convinced me
to pass over him as briefly as possible.

Hegel, challenged by Kant, sought to reconstruct metaphysics
so that it encompasses within it a philosophy of history. Hegel's
working axiom was this: "What is rational is real, and what is real
is rational." If everything that is real is also rational, then according to Hegel it can be known.

Hegel makes an important distinction that Kant does not: Hegel
sees reason and understanding as two completely different powers.
Understanding is not the same thing as reason, but is merely a particular function of reason. Understanding views everything in terms
of sharp contrasts. Understanding, as Kant supposed, is indeed
bounded by the finite and cannot gain absolute knowledge. But reason, says Hegel, is not so bounded. Indeed, human reason participates in infinite or absolute Reason. Hegel speaks of Reason with a
capital *R* as the Absolute Spirit, which is pure thought or absolute

knowledge. The world as we know it is in a kind of evolutionary or organic process. The Absolute Spirit works itself out in history.

Hegel saw history as the incarnation or dynamic unfolding of the Absolute Spirit. Man's mind is connected to the Absolute Spirit in such a way that it can be reached by human reason. We think about the Absolute in a way that is analogous to how the Absolute unfolds or expresses itself: by way of a dialectic process.

Hegel's Dialectic

The term *dialectic* refers to tension between ideas. Some have used it as a synonym for *contradiction,* which is tension with a vengeance. Hegel's dialectic process begins with a plausible starting point, which becomes a *thesis.* When analyzed, the thesis may imply a contradictory notion—an *antithesis.* This seeming contradiction tends to create an impasse, as did the philosophies of Heraclitus and Parmenides, and as did rationalism and empiricism.

The impasse can be resolved only by a *synthesis,* which in effect rescues what is true in both the thesis and the antithesis. Hegel sees this resolution through synthesis as the result of *Aufgehoben,* an elevating or lifting up of thought to a new level. Things progress in a triadic fashion (see fig. 10.2).

Figure 10.2
Hegel's Dialectic

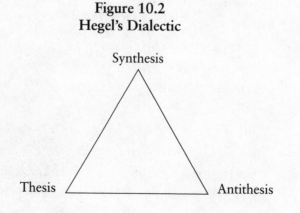

A synthesis is achieved, then it becomes a new thesis. This in turn engenders a new antithesis, which demands resolution in a new synthesis. History moves in this upward, progressive fashion, as seen in figure 10.3.

Figure 10.3
Hegel's View of History

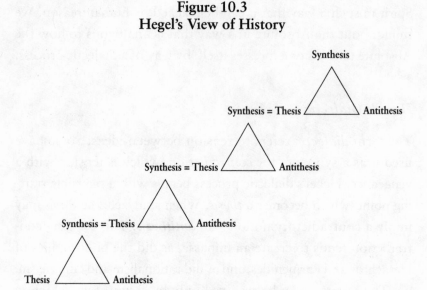

In anticipation of our look at Karl Marx, we could label Hegel's philosophy as "dialectical idealism." In dialectical fashion, truth and history evolve to a higher plane. Hegel illustrates this with his first triad of knowledge (see fig. 10.4). Being is the most

Figure 10.4
Hegel's First Triad

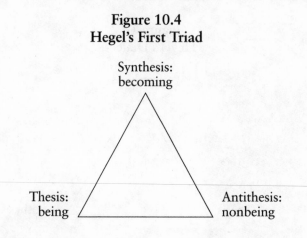

fundamental concept the mind can formulate. But the very concept of being contains within it its antithesis, the idea of nothing or nonbeing. As the mind wrestles with being and nonbeing, it moves to the concept of becoming. But this new synthesis rests on the prior notions of being and nonbeing.

For Hegel the history of the world is the history of nations, which progress not by chance but through a rational process. There is a reason, indeed Reason, behind all changes in history.

Karl Marx ranks as one of the most remarkable thinkers in history—remarkable for the degree to which and the rapidity with which his ideas had an impact on world culture. When I was in high school, the population of the world was 2 billion by the time I was forty-five the population had increased dramatically. What stunned me, however, was that by that time 2 billion people were living behind the Iron Curtain. By the time I was forty-five, as many people lived under Marxist regimes as had lived in the entire world when I was a teenager.

The philosophy of Marx, known popularly as dialectical materialism, represents a sharp contrast with Hegel's philosophy of history. Marx agrees with Hegel that the movement of history is dialectic in nature, but Marx insists that the force moving history is not ideals or reason but economics. The clash between rival economic views is the source of conflict and change. Marx was not satisfied, however, to sit at a table in the British Museum library and wait for nature to take its course. Changes could and should be imposed by men of action, who will generate revolutions.

Marx's Disillusionment

Marx was born in Trier, Germany, in 1818, about a century before the Russian Revolution, to Jewish parents. When Marx was a boy, the family moved to a German town that was predominantly

Lutheran. For business or economic reasons Karl's father "converted" to Lutheranism, fueling Karl's lifelong disillusionment with the role of religion in life.

By age twenty-three Marx had his Ph.D. in philosophy. He had read heavily in the works of Hegel and of Ludwig Feuerbach. Feuerbach had taught that man is not created in the image of God but God is created in the image of man. All theology, according to Feuerbach, is nothing more than anthropology. Marx embraced Feuerbach's idea that man, not God, realizes himself in history.

Marx's philosophy of history is at the same time a philosophy of man. Classicists defined man as *Homo sapiens,* "man the wise," believing that what separates man from beast is the human intellect. Marx redefines man as *Homo faber,* "man the maker" (the German word for "factory" is *fabrik*).

When meeting someone for the first time, we usually ask at least these three questions: 1) What is your name? 2) Where do you live? 3) What do you do? The third question concerns one's work or labor. This is the question that most concerns Marx because he sees man's identity bound up with his labor. For Marx labor is the primary catalyst for human self-realization. Man is unique because he makes his own activity the object of his consciousness and will. Labor is a dynamic process between man and nature. By his labor man survives.

The epochs of world history, says Marx, are determined not so much by *what* humans produce or make as by *how* they make it. Marx keenly understands the critical role played by tools in the production of goods. For example, why does the American farmer produce so much more grain than a farmer in an underdeveloped Third-World nation? Both farmers may be the same size, the same age, and of equal intelligence. But one uses John Deere machines to plant and harvest and drives his goods to market in an air-conditioned truck. The other uses a crude plow, harvests by hand, and takes his goods to market on the back of a donkey. One farmer owns the tools or the "means of production" and the other does not. This is the crucial difference between the two. The industrial revolution created tools that increased the production of goods exponentially.

Human community, according to Marx, is created by labor—more specifically, by the division of labor. People work for each other. Labor is a collective enterprise, making coexistence essential to survival. This cooperative venture of labor is what connects people to one another in world history.

Marx saw the industrial revolution as a serious threat to the well-being of humanity. Society changed dramatically from an agrarian to an industrial society as people left their farms in droves to seek employment in factories. In the words of a more recent song, "How are you going to keep them down on the farm?"

What did this mean for humanity? The shift from agrarianism to industrialism resulted in the worker's dehumanization. It created a state of economic estrangement, one that required and demanded some sort of reconciliation. The laborer, who as a farmer labored for himself, now had to sell his labor to the capitalist, who owned the means of production, the tools. In a pick-up baseball game with no umpire, the ruling of "safe" or "out" in the final analysis is made by whomever owns the bat or ball. "It's my bat, so you're out" is the rule. In this system, whoever owns the tools rules the game.

Even though the worker "willingly" leaves the farm to work in a factory and enters into a "free industrial contract" (earning wages for his labor), Marx sees this transaction as anything but "willing" and "free." The economic system "forces" the worker to abandon self-employment and to hire himself out to the capitalist as a wage-earner. In reality the worker, according to Marx, becomes merely a wage-earning *slave*. The worker's labor becomes a means to someone else's end. The worker no longer owns either the tools (the means of production) or the fruit of his labor (the products made).

The Worker's Alienation

In this process Marx discerned four distinct aspects of the worker's alienation: He is alienated from 1) nature, 2) himself, 3) his "species being," and 4) other beings.

Man's original relationship to nature is disrupted by his "unnatural" separation from the fruit of his labor. His labor becomes a commodity, something to be bought and sold. His labor is no longer his own.

On a fundamental level the worker loses his *ownership*. Marx understands that the economic power of capitalism lies in the matter of ownership. The worker owns nothing. Even a highly paid worker is, in Marx's judgment, merely a highly paid slave.

We see this drama worked out every day in our culture. The vast majority of people are workers rather than owners. Even salaried managerial employees receive wages for the tasks they undertake on behalf of the company. Not even executives, who may have very high salaries, own the company—unless they receive stock options. Marx did not foresee the extent to which workers could participate in ownership by investing a portion of their wages in stocks.

The essence of capitalism is to have your money work for you. You accumulate wealth even while you sleep. For example, the farmer who owns his farm may labor hard during the day to cultivate his crops. Yet while he sleeps his crops are growing, and (if nature is kind) his abundance is increasing.

In my own life I am both an employee and self-employed. As

an employee I am paid a salary for my labor. I am paid at a set rate regardless of the company's profit or loss. (This holds true, of course, only "up to a point": If the company fails to prosper, I may be out of a job.) I also write books. The lion's share of ownership of my books is in the hands of my publishers. I receive compensation for my relatively small portion of ownership by way of royalties. While writing this book, somewhere in the world a book I have previously written is earning royalties for me. I can also invest the income from these royalties in the stock market in hopes that my capital will increase.

With ownership, however, comes risk. He who owns something must invest his capital. That capital can increase or decrease—it can even be lost altogether. Every year in America, 500,000 new businesses are started. After one year 20 percent of them fail. After ten years only 4 percent still exist, indicating a huge rate of failure. Though the benefits of ownership are great, the risks are also great. It is usually safer to invest capital in strong, established enterprises than in start-up ventures.

The sports page is now filled with stories of litigation, holdouts, and so forth. Players (the workers in this case) demand a greater slice of ownership, but without having taken the original risk in creating a franchise.

Marx sees the worker being alienated from himself because his work is not voluntary. It is imposed on him, creating a feeling of dread. The worker is "blue" on Monday and cannot wait for Friday. The worker feels "human" only during his leisure hours. Man as *Homo faber* is no longer fulfilled in his work.

Man is alienated from his "species being" in the sense that human beings must express their character in free, conscious activity. Animals "produce" only to meet their most natural needs. The beaver builds his dam and the bird her nest, but man labors to produce far beyond his basic needs. He creates artistically, intellectually, and with a host of other productions. As a wage-earner, says Marx, man loses his creative freedom or it is stifled and, in a sense, he is reduced to an animal who labors simply to put bread on the table.

Finally, the worker experiences estrangement from other people. The fellowship *(mit-mensch)* of common labor for common ownership is lost. Capitalism emphasizes private property and reduces ownership to the few. Under communism, as Marx envisioned it, everyone labors together for the common good and everyone owns everything. The problem, of course, is that when everyone owns everything, no one owns anything.

Society's Substructure

According to Marx, every society has both a substructure and a superstructure. A substructure is like the foundation for a building, while the superstructure is like the building itself. The foundation or substructure determines the kind of superstructure that can be erected on it.

A society's substructure is its economic basis or material order, including the factors of production and the relations of production. Historically the relations of production have changed from slave to feudal to capitalist systems. The way tools are developed determines the way men relate to each other. The stone ax or the bow and arrow allow a kind of independent existence. The plow demands a division of labor. Heavy machinery increases the division of labor. The more sophisticated the tools, the greater the division of labor. This increased division of labor escalates class struggle.

Capitalism, according to Marx, reduces the classes to two: the owners (the bourgeoisie) and the workers (the proletariat) (he did not anticipate the rise of a strong middle class). The value system created by this system effects a higher degree of estrangement. What Marx means by *values* is not the common contemporary meaning, which confuses values with ethics and morality. Value can be distinguished from ethics, though ultimately the two cannot be separated. In economic theory value is subjective, involving personal preferences. No other person can declare what a good or service is worth to me. I may value chocolate ice cream more than you do, and you may value vanilla ice cream more than I do.

The subjective nature of value drives exchanges in the marketplace, either by bartering or by using currency. In barter a man who has an excess of shoes and a shortage of lamps may trade with a man who has an excess of lamps and a shortage of shoes. When goods and services are purchased with money, this is merely a more complex form of barter. In a free transaction, when the seller asks a higher price for his goods than the buyer is willing to pay, the transaction fails. If I value the radio you are selling more than the money I have to spend, I will buy the radio. If I value my money more than your radio, I will not purchase it.

In capitalism the price of goods and services, as well as the cost of labor, is determined by the market forces of supply and demand. The larger the labor force, the cheaper the cost of labor. This allows the products to be sold at a price higher than the cost of labor (and materials), which results in a profit. This profit is then gained by the owner. This creates what Marx calls *surplus value*. The fact that the owner gains more value from his produce than the value of the labor that produced it Marx sees as an exploitation of the laboring class. This exploitation is a necessary ingredient of capitalism and fuels what Marx calls the "iron law of wages."

In contrast to capitalism's market value of labor, Marx argues for the *labor theory of value:* The value of a product is based on the amount of labor put into it. If any single principle of Marxism led to its abysmal failure, it was Marx's labor theory of value. To seek such an objective theory of value is to oppose the very nature of humanity with its individual tastes, wants, and needs. In the capitalist system prices are driven by what people value, what they want to have. Rembrandt could paint a picture of an orange much more quickly and efficiently than I can. I have to work harder and longer to paint an orange than Rembrandt did. But in the marketplace most people will pay far more money for Rembrandt's painting than they will for mine. The quality of a good or service cannot be determined simply by how much labor has gone into it.

Marx predicted that the condition of workers in capitalist societies would become steadily worse. The poor would become poorer while the rich would become richer, until the masses would revolt and take over the means of production for themselves.

This was Marx's greatest error. He assumed the myth that the rich can only get rich at the expense of the poor. One man's gain must spell another man's loss. That may be true in a poker game, but not in the real world of business. With the increase of production by better tools, the cost per unit of goods declines (through the law of supply and demand). This makes it easier for people to receive the goods and services, and it raises the poor person's standard of living. No economic system has been as effective as capitalism in raising the human standard of living.

Society's Superstructure

Marx argues that the shape and style of a society's superstructure is determined by the economic substructure on which it is built. This superstructure includes society's ideology in such areas as religion, morality, and law. A society's "thinking" therefore flows out of its "materialistic base." Neither reason nor theology shapes society; rather, society's economic platform shapes its reason or theology.

In the realm of law, for example, Marx argues that law is established, not on a religious, philosophical, or natural foundation, but on the vested interests of the ruling class. In capitalism the law serves to defend bourgeois interests. On the one hand Marx can be seen as a prophet of our acceptance of lobbying groups that openly work for legislation favoring their interests. On the other hand he failed to foresee that a "proletariat" majority could hit the minority bourgeoisie with a progressive income tax. Marx did see that economics can easily be politicized by laws that tend to reflect some group's vested interests rather than an abstract concept of justice.

Within Marxism, equality is more important than equity. Indeed Marxism assumes that equity is served only by equality. This means that the sluggard or indolent "deserves" or is "entitled" to an equal share of the pie with the diligent and laborious. This embodies the principle, "From each according to his ability, to each according to his need."

Likewise, according to Marx, religion, the "opiate of the masses," is a narcotic used by the ruling class to keep the proletariat in line. The slave is promised a reward in heaven ("pie in the sky") if he behaves now and keeps his fingers out of the bourgeoisie's pie. This idea was echoed by Vladimir Lenin. He said that Communists take it for granted that there is no God. But if there were, it would be but one more reason to fight him, so evil are the works attributed to him. For Marx (and later Lenin) the church serves no purpose other than as a museum harboring the relics of the Middle Ages.

Many attempts have been made to create a synthesis between Marxism and religion. This can be achieved only by turning

Marxism itself into a religion, for its fundamental thesis is irreconcilable with historical Judaeo-Christianity.

Marx's eschatology, based on his dialectical view of history, predicts the following chain reaction:

1. Capitalism will move into a period of overproduction.
2. Wages will be reduced.
3. The worker's purchasing power will be reduced.
4. A surplus of goods will be created.
5. A war will be started to use up the surplus.
6. Postwar stress will end in the system's self-destruction.

Marx's ultimate goal was to end private ownership through the state's ownership of the means of production. This would yield the utopian order of a classless society, a dream shattered in the Soviet Union and in Maoist China.

11

Søren Kierkegaard:
Danish Gadfly

One of the questions I am asked most frequently is, "What is existentialism?" When I reply glibly, "Existentialism is a philosophy of existence," I am met with puzzled looks and blank stares. Rightly so. To define existentialism as a philosophy of existence is not very helpful. The term *existentialism* has been used so loosely in our culture that Jean-Paul Sartre complained it had lost its meaning entirely.

Existentialism is extremely difficult to explain, due largely to its suffix, *ism*. Attaching *ism* to the end of a word usually indicates a system of thought, but existentialism tends to be strongly anti-system. Though we find common threads of concern among so-called existentialist philosophers, it may be prudent to speak of existentialists rather than of existentialism. On the other hand, some philosophers who wear the label *existentialist* have constructed some rather elaborate systems.

We have seen the dramatic impact Marxist philosophy has had on the world. In the comprehensiveness and rapidity of its impact on Western culture, existentialism rivals Marxism. One cannot spend an active day in the Western world without encountering some aspect of existentialism. We are bombarded by it in novels, pop music, movies, television shows, religion, and every other part of life. In one sense existential thought has brought with it the conquest of the many over the one, of diversity over unity. In existentialism, becoming tends to swallow up being; the finite, the infinite; the temporal, the eternal; and the secular, the sacred.

Our culture reflects a peculiar form of secularism. We frequently use the word *secular* to mean "the realm outside the borders of the church." But when the suffix *ism* is added, the term *secular* means something far more radical.

In antiquity, Latin had at least two words that can be translated "world": *mundus* and *saeculum*. *Mundus* refers specifically to the physical dimensions or spatial aspects of this planet. From *mundus* we derive the word *mundane*. We remember the epitaph of Athanasius: "*Athanasius contra mundum,*" "Athanasius against the world." The Latin term *saeculum* refers to this world's temporal dimension, the "now" of the "here and now" *(hic et nunc)*.

In modern categories of secularism, the root idea is that this temporal world is all that there is. No transcendent, eternal realm exists. We are locked into this time and cannot escape. The jingle that captures this thought is, "You only go around once." In Kantian terms, the secularist lives with reference only to the phenomenal realm; all access to the noumenal is barred.

This pessimistic spirit of secularism is not shared by all existential philosophers. Since the nineteenth century there have been several notable religious existentialists, such as Karl Jaspers, Martin Buber, and especially Søren Kierkegaard. At the same time there have been numerous attempts to create a synthesis between existential philosophy and theology (as in the work of Paul Tillich and Rudolf Bultmann) and dialectical theology (as in the work of Karl Barth and Emil Brunner).

One reason existential philosophy has had such a dramatic and rapid impact on modern culture is that in many respects it has eliminated the middleman. The middleman who typically translates abstract and technical philosophy to the populace is the artist. It is no accident that the history of art, music, and drama follows the history of philosophy. The artist picks up new philosophical ideas, employs them, and communicates them as part of a particular artistic movement.

In the case of existentialism, however, some of its most forceful proponents were both philosophers and artists. For example, Jean-Paul Sartre wrote as a technical philosopher in *Being and Nothingness*[1] and as a playwright in *No Exit*.[2] Others, such as Albert Camus and Søren Kierkegaard, were gifted literary artists who could carry their heavy philosophical messages directly to the people.

Another Gadfly

As Socrates was the "gadfly of Athens," so Søren Kierkegaard was nicknamed "the Danish gadfly." Kierkegaard, popularly known as the father of modern existentialism, is credited with having coined the term *existentialism*.

In many respects Kierkegaard was a tragic figure. His father seduced a servant girl shortly before his wife died. He later married the girl and had seven children by her, the last being Søren, born in 1813. Affected by a morbid guilt for his sinful life, Søren's father imposed on his children a rigorous religious training.

As a young man Søren was something of a bon vivant, noted for his repartee. A crisis caused him to break his engagement to his beloved Regina and to write his first book, *Either/Or*.[3] In this book he expresses the crossroads he faced: to regress to a life of sensual debauchery or to pursue spiritual integrity with passion.

Kierkegaard was given to severe melancholy, and his brilliant insights and beautiful literary style grew out of his personal pain. He once recounted the ancient myth of a knave sentenced to be burned at the stake. The soft-hearted king was unable to bear the screams of the tormented, but while the knave was burning, his piercing screams were transformed by fickle muses into beautiful music. When the king heard only soothing music, he told the executioner to put more wood on the fire so the music would continue.

On another occasion Kierkegaard told of a clown who worked in a theatre. When fire broke out backstage, the clown was sent out to warn the audience. His cries of alarm were met with laughter from the audience, who assumed he was jesting. The more he shouted "Fire!" the more the people laughed.

These stories convey Kierkegaard's sentiment concerning the plight of the artist. Only through suffering can the artist create beauty that "entertains" others, but his cries of pathos are greeted as the king received the screams of the knave and as the audience received the warning of the clown. Kierkegaard died in 1855 at age forty-two.

The Three Stages

In his early work Kierkegaard notes three "stages along life's way," or *stadia* of human existence. These represent optional lifestyles people can choose.

First is the *aesthetic stage,* the defining characteristic of which is that one lives life as a spectator. The spectator engages in social life and can discuss the arts with brilliance, but he is incapable of openness in human relationships and lacks self-direction. He is chiefly an observer rather than a doer or actor. Kierkegaard defines this as a condition of spiritual impotence that leads to sin and personal despair. The person leaves the meaning of life itself to the mercy of external events. He looks for fulfillment and escape from boredom in amusements. In a sense the aesthetic stage is a form of hedonism, in which life consists in emotional and sensual experiences.

Kierkegaard distinguishes between spirit and sensuousness.

Using a house as a metaphor, he calls the building the spirit, and the cellar or basement sensuousness. The person living in the aesthetic stage prefers to live in the cellar, but life in the cellar cannot result in true existence. Finding himself in the cellar with all its fatal attractions, he must choose to leave it by an act of the will, with an existential "decision."

Second is the *ethical stage*. Here a person moves from personal preference and taste to recognizing and embracing universal rules of conduct. He acquires a sense of moral responsibility and submits himself to laws. But he is also gripped by rational norms, laws that appear only in the abstract. He experiences conflict with guilt and becomes aware of his finitude and estrangement from God.

The moral law imposes a kind of objectivity in which the universal dominates the individual. In this context Kierkegaard

Figure 11.1
Three Stages of Life

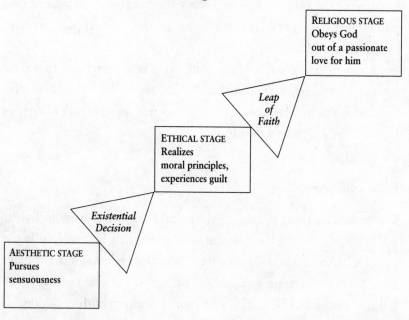

rages against the supreme rationalism of Hegel. Hegel submerges the individual, virtually annihilating him with the universal or the absolute. Universal essence swallows up particular existence. Seeking to live simply by law, one loses the personal in abstract social and legal relationships. When a person believes he can attain righteousness simply by fulfilling the letter of the law, then the ethical becomes an obstacle to faith. The reality of guilt places the person in a new situation of either/or: He either remains at the ethical stage or makes a transition out of it to the third stage or highest stadium, the *religious stage*.

The religious stage, however, cannot be reached merely by thought. The person must make a decisive act of commitment, what Kierkegaard calls a leap: the leap of faith. This is a subjective matter that requires the person to exercise passion.

At one point Kierkegaard, in evaluating the culture of nineteenth-century Europe, says his complaint is, not that his age is wicked, but that it is paltry, lacking in passion. When discouraged, he turns to the Old Testament, where men lie, steal, cheat, murder, and commit adultery. These are real people of real passion who seek faith amid anguish.

Kierkegaard's leap of faith lands one in the lap, not of a God who can be known philosophically or rationally, but of one who himself is the supreme subject. God is not an abstract *it* but, as Buber later emphasized, a *thou*.

Fear and Trembling

Kierkegaard's most pressing existential question is how to live as a Christian. The clearest example of true faith he can find is the patriarch Abraham. In *Fear and Trembling*[4] Kierkegaard considers Abraham's struggle to obey God's unthinkable command to kill his son Isaac (Gen. 22). The pain Abraham endures in deciding to obey is not unlike Kierkegaard's pain in renouncing his love for Regina.

As Kierkegaard muses over the story of Abraham and Isaac, he asks, "Is there such a thing as a teleological suspension of the ethical?"[5] That is, can the ethical ever be temporarily suspended for the sake of a higher power?

In reflecting on Abraham's dilemma, Kierkegaard looks at the text in which God says to Abraham, "Take now your son, your only son Isaac, whom you love . . ." (Gen. 22:2). The precision of the command is unbearable. Abraham's greatest blessing is Isaac, the child of Abraham and Sarah's old age, the child of promise. In an attempt to fulfill the divine promise, Abraham had earlier fathered a son by Sarah's handmaiden, Hagar. God had rejected Ishmael as the child of promise and banished him to the wilderness. Now God says, "Take your son. . . ." If that were the extent of the command, Abraham could sacrifice Ishmael and spare Isaac. But God is specific. He requires Abraham's "only son," the one "whom you love."

In *Fear and Trembling* Kierkegaard keeps coming back to the narrative that declares, "So Abraham rose early in the morning . . ." (Gen. 22:3). Kierkegaard has little time for interpreters who believe Abraham is a paper saint who diligently arises to do his duty. Kierkegaard's Abraham tosses and turns all night in bitter anguish, struggling in his soul with the command and questioning if it is truly from God. Abraham lived before God gave Moses the Decalogue at Sinai, including the commandment, "Thou shalt not kill." But Abraham clearly has the moral law written on his heart and cannot fathom the dialectic (the conflict) before him.

Martin Luther's beloved wife once said to her husband that she could not believe the story of Abraham and Isaac because God would never treat a son like that. "But Katie," Luther replied, "he *did* treat his son like that."

Abraham obeyed God in a passionate act of faith. He went beyond the ethical stage to the religious stage by acting out of trust in his personal relationship with God. A life marked by risk includes real fear and trembling, dread and anxiety.

Kierkegaard's portrayal of the religious stage is no brief for antinomianism or ethical relativism. Obedience to God is required. As Jesus remarked, "If you love Me, keep My commandments" (John 14:15). Obedience is motivated, not by a zeal for conformity to abstract precepts but by a passionate love for the lawgiver who says, "Thou shalt." Obedience flows out of spontaneous love, not external coercion. Nor was Kierkegaard saying that only the "spirit" of the law is important. To reject the letter of the law while keeping its spirit is no better than to keep the letter of the law while ignoring its spirit.

Kierkegaard's point is that the Christian life flows out of the deepest passions of a person amid risk and anxiety.

An Attack on Christendom

Kierkegaard reacted strongly against the state church and nominal Christianity. Hegel's synthesis of church and state, according to Kierkegaard, had produced the arid Christianity of "citizen Christians." In Denmark people were considered to be Christians simply because they were Danes, obscuring the call to individual faith and conversion. For writing *Attack upon "Christendom,"*[6] Kierkegaard fully expected to be arrested and prosecuted. He argued that the state church had reduced Christianity to an empty formalism and externalism, which in effect produces mere spectators to true Christianity. This critique reflects Kierkegaard's most important philosophical thesis, which may be called *truth as subjectivity.*

Kierkegaard's view of truth is the root of much controversy.

He believes in the axiom that God is truth. But he argues that the believer finds truth only when he experiences the tension between himself and God. Is he saying that truth itself is merely a matter of subjective belief? Or is he arguing that truth is known only when grasped in the inward experience of the believing subject? If he means the former, then he would be the father of modern relativism.

Kierkegaard does declare that "Truth is subjectivity." This implies more than that truth has a subjective element: It suggests a wholesale rejection of objective truth.

But that Kierkegaard probably did not intend a wholesale rejection of objective truth may be seen in his declaration that "What is out there is an objective uncertainty." It is one thing to say that we do not achieve objective certainty about external reality; it is another thing to say that there is no objective reality out there.

Kierkegaard's subjective method stresses the importance of personal experience over factual information. The subjective apprehension of truth by faith is the kind of experience that deeply influences how we live. Kierkegaard would reject Descartes' method of inferring existence from thought. For Kierkegaard, thought moves existence *away from* the real. One moves not from an "idea" to the real but from the real to the idea. An abstract concept of a chair or "chairness" actually abrogates or eliminates actual chairs, because the particular characteristics of a real, particular chair (its weight, color, style, and so forth) are lost in or obscured by the abstraction. This is why Kierkegaard is called an existentialist. He is concerned not with abstract essences (metaphysics) but with concrete, particular existence.

What is at stake with Kierkegaard's view of truth as subjectivity is nothing less than the classical Christian view of *objective historicity*. Biblical Christianity is tied to real history. Christianity affirms crucial events that actually happened, objectively, in the fullness of time. If dehistoricized, Christianity is destroyed.

Modern existential theology has taken this to an extreme. These theologians say it does not matter whether or not there was a real historical Jesus. What matters is the existential impact of "Easter faith" on believers. For existentialists such as Rudolf Bultmann, Christianity manifests itself not on the horizontal plane of history but always in the *hic et nunc* (the here and now) as a matter of decision. Bultmann developed a theology of timelessness in which God meets us "directly and immediately from above."

An Unscientific Postscript

In his *Concluding Unscientific Postscript*[7] Kierkegaard tells of two men in prayer. One is a church member who professes an orthodox view of God but prays to God with a false spirit. In truth, Kierkegaard says, he is praying to an idol. The other man is a heathen who prays to idols with true passion. Therefore, says Kierkegaard, he is praying to God. Why? Because truth is found in the inward how, not the external what. This passionate inwardness becomes the highest truth for the individual.

But this begs the question, If a man worships Satan with inward passion, does this make him a Christian? It is difficult for me to imagine that this is what Kierkegaard means, yet at times this certainly seems to be what he affirms. "An objective uncertainty, held fast through appropriation with the most passionate inwardness," he says in *Concluding Unscientific Postscript,* "is the truth, the highest truth there is for an existing individual."[8] If we were to apply this thesis to the world of competing philosophies, we could conclude that a zealous passion for Hegel's philosophy makes Hegel's philosophy true and Kierkegaard's false.

Elsewhere Kierkegaard says that an objective acceptance of

Christianity is either paganism or thoughtlessness. If he means that a *merely* objective acceptance of Christianity without a subjective, passionate commitment is pagan, then, "No harm, no foul." If he means that believing Christianity's truth claims to be objectively true is pagan, then Kierkegaard fouls out of the game.

An inherent weakness of the subjective method is that it remains dependent on constantly renewed experiences. The anchor for the soul has no rope. While stressing the paradoxes of Christianity that one must embrace by faith, Kierkegaard goes too far by excluding reason too completely. Christianity may contain mystery and paradox, but it is not irrational. If the leap of faith is a leap into the absurd, it is fatal. Scripture calls us to leap out of the darkness into the light—it is not a leap into the darkness where one hopes that God is waiting with a net.

Kierkegaard distinguishes between the "indicative" and the "imperative," between what man actually is and what he ought to be. There is a movement from a person's essential condition to his existential condition. This movement, says Kierkegaard, is described in the theology of the Fall. Sin cuts a person off from his essential humanity and plunges him into his current condition—estrangement from God. One's true essence is realized or actualized only by the leap of faith, by entering the religious stage of life where purity of heart is to will one thing—the passionate love of God.

Kierkegaard's rejection of Hegel and rational philosophy is not unrelated to Immanuel Kant. We remember that Kant saw a barrier between the phenomenal and noumenal worlds. This wall, according to Kant, is so wide that you can't go around it, so deep that you can't get under it, and so high that by theoretical thought you can't climb over it. Kierkegaard found his way over the wall—by his leap of faith.

If Kierkegaard emerged as the father of Christian existentialism, he was rivaled in the nineteenth century by Friedrich Nietzsche, an atheistic existentialist. The history of existential philosophy since these two men tends to grow from these two radically different roots. Seventy-five years after his death, Kierkegaard's work was rediscovered and revived by such continental theologians as Karl Barth and Emil Brunner. Their "neo-orthodox" or "dialectical" theology captured the Western theological scene. Brunner's little book *Truth as Encounter*[9] puts flesh on the bones of Kierkegaard's view of truth as subjectivity.

12

Friedrich Nietzsche:
Atheistic Existentialist

Graffiti seen on a subway wall in New York City makes this announcement:

> "God is dead." —Nietzsche
> "Nietzsche is dead." —God

The movement dubbed "theothanatology" ("the science of the death of God") finds its roots in Friedrich Nietzsche. But Nietzsche's philosophical labor goes far beyond writing an epitaph for God or inspiring, as some claim, Adolf Hitler's mad dream of creating an Aryan super-race of blonde-haired, blue-eyed Nazis. (It is alleged that the Bavarian housepainter, before becoming führer of the Third Reich, gave copies of *Thus Spake Zarathustra*[1] at Christmas to his brown-shirt cronies.)

Nietzsche was born in 1844, the grandson of a Lutheran clergyman. Friedrich was named after the king of Prussia. The boy's father died when he was only four, and he was reared in an extended family of women: his mother, his sister, his grandmother, and two spinster aunts. Some may speculate that he was subjected to Clintonesque "child abuse" by being caught in a gaggle of quarreling women, but this would be mere revisionism or journalistic redaction. In fact, Nietzsche displayed a prodigious intellectual capacity as a young man, and he was appointed a professor at the University of Basel at the age of twenty-four.

Before his falling out with Richard Wagner (Hitler's favorite composer), Nietzsche came under the spell of Wagner's Teutonic music. "When one wants to rid oneself of an intolerable pressure, one needs hashish," Nietzsche once remarked. "Well, I needed Wagner." Nietzsche's brief life (he died in 1900 at the age of fifty-six) was marked by repeated, serious health problems. At thirty-four he left his university post due to illness and roamed Europe looking for a cure. He spent his last eleven years in an asylum, undergoing treatment for a hopelessly incurable insanity, apparently caused by a severe infection of the brain. During this period he suffered such delusions that he identified himself with Jesus Christ, signing his letters, "The Crucified One." It is said that his sister, who was partly responsible for his continued care, sold tickets to people who wanted a firsthand glimpse of her famous but now-demented brother.

If one word captures the *Zeitgeist* of nineteenth-century Europe, it is *evolution*. The idea of evolution was not restricted to the realm of biology but was integral to several emerging philosophies of history, such as those of Hegel and Marx, and to Herbert Spencer's "social Darwinism." Some have dubbed Nietzsche the "philosopher of evolution." He himself rejected much of Darwin's thought but nevertheless was heavily influenced by him. Nietzsche extended the evolutionary hypothesis beyond the physical development of animals, making religion, philosophy, and logic the products of evolution. Yet he challenged the idea that mankind is locked into an upward spiral of progress. Evolution, for Nietzsche, does not occur according to some teleological plan (which involves a remnant of the idea of God); it is haphazard and, especially in the case of humans, does not always favor the advance of superior specimens, often thwarting it instead.

Like Kierkegaard, Nietzsche rejected the Hegelian ideal and saw the culture of nineteenth-century Europe not as advancing but as declining. Kierkegaard had complained that his age was paltry, lacking passion; Nietzsche complained that his age was decadent. Decadence is a process, perhaps an evolutionary one, though in this case the term *devolutionary* is more appropriate. Decadence, as the word connotes, is a process not of growth but of decay, not of generation but of degeneration.

Nietzsche blames much of this decay on Christianity's negative influence. With its emphasis on meekness and submission to deity, says Nietzsche, the Judaeo-Christian tradition squashes the fundamental spirit of humanity. Weakness replaces strength, and pity replaces boldness and courage.

Like Kierkegaard, Nietzsche is an existential philosopher. But where Kierkegaard is seen as the father of religious existentialism, Nietzsche is viewed as the father of atheistic existentialism. When declaring the death of God, Nietzsche attributes the deity's demise to a fatal dose of pity. "God is dead," Nietzsche declares, "He died of pity." Nietzsche says satirically that first there were many gods, such as those that inhabited Olympus; then monotheism emerged when one of the gods (the Jewish Yahweh) stood up and said, "Thou shalt have no other gods before me." At this point, says Nietzsche, all the other gods died—of laughter.

While working on his doctoral dissertation, Nietzsche studied classical Greek art and philosophy. He noted the ancient conflict seen in the images of Apollo and Dionysius. In these images Nietzsche discovered the visceral antagonism within himself, an antithesis between the mind and the will. In Apollo the rational and the orderly are incarnated. Apollo represents the Greek ideal of order and harmony. Apollonian art displays perfect symmetry and proportionality. Its sculpture displays no warts. The figure of Dionysius, on the other hand, represents the element of the chaotic. Dionysius was worshiped in the ancient Bacchanalia, named after Bacchus, god of the grape or of wine. In the ancient ritual, one attains mystical release from the inhibition of reason by entering into a drunken, orgiastic stupor. In this Dionysian frenzy a person loses his individual identity as he merges into mystical union with a transcendent "one" or "oversoul."

For Nietzsche the Apollonian ideal is realized in Hegel's intellectualism, the Dionysian mood in Arthur Schopenhauer's voluntarism. The Dionysian model offers entrance into a dynamic stream of life-force marked by passion and expressed in music that creates a feeling of abandon.

Sometimes Nietzsche is portrayed as having chosen the Dionysian model over that of Apollo, but this is incorrect. Rather, Nietzsche believes that the great achievement of Greek culture is its marrying of the two elements. What he decries in modern culture is the wholesale denial of the Dionysian element and its legitimacy. He blames Christianity for banishing Dionysius from public respectability and leaving the world with an idealism that fundamentally denies a critical life-force for human fulfillment and authentic human existence.

The Will to Power

Nietzsche thought that Darwin attached too much significance to the natural law of self-preservation. Simple self-preservation or the survival of the species cannot "save the phenomena" of nature. Frequently in nature, the power to create new forms brings death rather than life. The most fundamental force in life is not self-preservation, according to Nietzsche, but is what he calls the *will to power.*

The will to power may be linked to modern paradigms such as

people's attempts to rise to the top of the pyramid, an adult version of "King of the Hill." In psychological categories the will to power is the aspiration for significance, the search for "meaning" in one's life. People want their lives to count for something. The pursuit of dignity and status may reflect such aspirations. From a Christian perspective the will to power is the noble aspiration for significance run amok.

Darwin's view is too passive for Nietzsche. Darwin stresses the process of adaptation to environment and environmental changes. Nietzsche insists that life is active; it exerts power and moves toward growth and expansion. Life is not about mere survival or preserving the status quo.

The difference may be seen in the business world. Corporations are successful only when they continue to grow and expand. When a company enters a "maintenance mode," attempting to protect its current position, it has in effect decided to liquidate—it simply has not yet set a date for it. The urge to self-preservation is merely the result of a distressed condition. The will to power, on the other hand, struggles to produce more, at a faster rate, and more often. One life is lived at the expense of another. For someone to win the power struggle, someone must lose. There can be no conqueror without the conquered or the vanquished. Nature is not neat and clean, but wasteful and dirty.

The will to power, according to Nietzsche, is really a will to overpower. "The strongest and highest will to life does not find expression in a miserable struggle for existence, but in a will to war." Absolute moral rules such as those imposed by Christianity and Judaism are inhuman and dehumanizing; their ideal of peace denies man's most fundamental drive. These religions declare sinful that which is most natural to mankind. Their alienation of man from his basic nature yields only "botched and bungled" lives.

The Herd Morality

Nietzsche distinguishes between "herd morality" and "master morality." The former, also called slave morality, is the morality of those who seek security. It originates in the meanest and lowest elements of society—the weak, the oppressed, and those lacking in confidence. It elevates the "virtues" that help alleviate pain and affliction: sympathy, patience, kindness, humility, and so forth (these qualities sound a lot like what Galatians 5 calls the fruit of the Holy Spirit).

Slave or herd morality, for Nietzsche, is one of utility. (Utilitarianism is the social ethic that seeks the greatest good for the greatest number, sacrificing the desires of the few, or the superior, for the desires of the many.) Slave morality benefits the weak. Those who embrace it are like cattle or mindless sheep, seeking comfort and security in the herd or the flock. This morality is rooted in and driven by fear.

Historically, herd morality has succeeded by exacting revenge against superior masters. It defines the qualities of strong and courageous men as vices: He who accumulates wealth is greedy, and he who achieves power is a tyrant.

Master morality, according to Nietzsche, stands in strong contrast to slave morality. The master marches to a different drummer. Master morality is noble in that it is the morality of the nobility. To the noble, evil is that which is vulgar, pedestrian, and plebeian. The authentic patrician, unlike the plebe, believes that he creates his own values and morality. He is the master of his fate; he controls his destiny. He does not depend on the group for approval of his actions; he is his own judge. He seeks his own glory as he works out his will to power. He is the master stag who defeats all who lock horns with him. He holds power in high esteem and gives honor only to strength. He demands the most of himself, tackling rigorous tasks that only increase his strength.

Historically, says Nietzsche, the noble caste was found among barbarians. Before exhibiting their physical dominance over people, they developed the psychic strength to exercise their will to power. They were complete or authentic men. The barbarians finally lost out, however, because the masses succeeded in elevating ideals like peace and equality to the level of societal norms. With the advent of herd morality, man's most basic nature was denied, which in Nietzsche's view is a denial of life itself.

This triumph of the herd, according to Nietzsche, was based in the final analysis on dishonesty. The chief architects of this dishonesty were adherents of Judaism and Christianity. "I regard Christianity," Nietzsche once remarked, "as the most fatal and seductive lie that has ever yet existed—as the greatest and most impious lie." If Protagoras believed that "man is the measure of all things," Nietzsche declared that the morality of paltry people has become the measure of all things. In the name of God, New Testament ethics had been imposed on Western civilization, resulting in degeneracy.

For example, Christianity advocates the love of one's enemies, while nature requires that we hate our enemies since they are obstacles to our individual will to power. Thus Christianity dilutes the vital energy of strong men by subverting their natural biological instincts. These men are emasculated by inserting "God" into the equation. Christianity succeeds in provoking a hatred of the earth and earthly things.

In calling for a reevaluation of morals, Nietzsche is not asking for a new system of morality based on absolute norms; he rejects all such systems. Rather, he calls for a revolt against the entrenched herd morality, for unmasking it and exposing its hypocrisy. It must be shown that what herd morality deems "good" is not real virtue but merely a guise for weakness. Life is will to power and nothing else. Man must be free to exercise his own nature.

It is odd that Nietzsche complains about the "dishonesty" of traditional morality. Apparently he thinks honesty is a transcendent virtue that is normative even for the master. But what if honesty conflicts with one's will to power? Then it too must give way. Even while attacking herd morality, Nietzsche retreats behind one of the virtues he is trying to overcome.

The Superman

Nietzsche's superman *(Übermensch)* is nothing like the comic-book hero. Nietzsche does not have in view the mild-mannered reporter for the *Daily Planet*. Nietzsche's superman has nothing to do with Jimmy Olson, Lois Lane, or a grumbling editor who constantly exclaims, "Great Caesar's Ghost!" Nor is Nietzsche's superman vulnerable to kryptonite. His superman does not need to be faster than a speeding bullet, more powerful than a locomotive, or able to leap tall buildings in a single bound.

Nietzsche's superman is a conqueror. Nature is vindicated, not by the masses who are merely able to survive, but by the few gifted persons who are geniuses and supermen. Supermen are not found in some future race cultivated by Aryan programs. They are simply superior individuals such as have appeared from time to time throughout history. They include such figures as Julius Caesar, Alexander the Great, and Napoléon Bonaparte.

Nietzsche describes the superman as an individual of supreme courage—"dialectical courage." This is the courage that exists and is exerted amid contradictory tension. Nietzsche is often regarded as the father of nihilism, which asserts that there is no ultimate meaning to human existence, no transcendent purpose, value, or virtue. In the final analysis there is only the *nihil—das Nicht*—"the nothingness of human existence." In this scenario there are no virtues. Ultimately courage itself is meaningless. For this reason Nietzsche calls his own idea of courage "dialectical," for it operates in the realm of contradiction. The obvious question is, Why be courageous if courage is meaningless? Nietzsche would reply, "Be courageous anyway!"

Nietzsche's superman, who is supremely courageous, is the man who, knowing that there are no values, creates his own. He sails his ship into uncharted waters and builds his house on the slopes of Vesuvius. He is the Ernest Hemingway hero, the matador who defies life and grabs the bull by the horns, the old man who takes on the sea alone. He is James Cagney in *The White Cliffs of Dover,* who, after a bloody dogfight in the sky, steers his crippled plane into the sheer wall of the white cliffs, spitting at the enemy through the shattered glass of the cockpit window as the screen fades to black. Of course, on the morrow the sun is shining serenely on the calm repose of the chalky cliffs and the birds are twittering, while the corpse of the pilot and the wreckage of his plane are entombed under fathoms of water at the bottom of the sea.

Nietzsche's superman exhibits a balance between the Apollonian and Dionysian elements. He is not a result of evolutionary progress, which suggests a linear movement of history; Nietzsche opts instead for an adaptation of ancient cyclical views of history. The movie *They Shoot Horses, Don't They?* depicts a marathon dance contest during the Depression, when people did strange things for entertainment or to earn a dollar. To quicken the pace and force more couples to drop out of the marathon, the master of ceremonies calls a promenade, which requires the couples to move double-time around the dance floor's perimeter. The emcee, in diabolical tones, chants into the microphone: "Round

and round and round they go. Where they stop, nobody knows."
The promenade is a grueling exercise for the contestants, one of
whom suffers a fatal heart attack. This film drips with the motif of
existential philosophy. It graphically portrays the despair produced by a cyclical view of time. The same theme is featured in the
Old Testament book of Ecclesiastes, which contrasts life "under
the sun" (for the perspective of this world) with life "under
heaven." The view that yields despair and the ultimate futility (the
"vanity of vanities") is the one of the endless cycle of sunsets and
sunrises *(The Sun Also Rises),* the one in which there is nothing
new under the sun.

Nietzsche argues that if evolution had a goal, surely it would
have been recycled by now. Time is infinite, causing the constant
recurrence of world states. The French Revolution will happen
again and again, always producing a figure like Napoléon. The
real world is an endless sea of becoming. The only apparent general trend is the manifestation of the will to power.

Part of this eternal recurrence, says Nietzsche, is the necessity of the death of God. "God" is merely an illusion about the
absolute, an illusion created by the human mind. This illusion
must be shattered for the new age of the superman to dawn. Those
who have created God must murder him. We must deliberately
eliminate from our thinking the very idea of God. Then the world
system of morality and standards that relies on this idea for its
existence will be destroyed.

Nietzsche's protagonist, Zarathustra, descends from his
mountain to declare the awful yet glad tidings of God's death.
Those who heed this declaration realize that they live in the
shadow of a dead God and fear the consequence of nihilism. God
is not to be believed, because he is no longer believable, nor is he
worthy of human support. "That we find no God—either in history or in nature or behind nature—is not what differentiates us,

but that we experience what has been revered as God, not as 'god-like' but as miserable, as absurd, as harmful, not merely as an error but as a crime against life," Nietzsche writes. "We deny god as God. If one were to prove this God of the Christians to us, we should be even less able to believe in him."

The "Logic" of Nietzsche

Any evaluation of Nietzsche's thought must inquire into his epistemology. How does one refute a philosopher who declares absurdity at the outset? When dealing with apostles of irrationality, I always ask them why they even bother to talk. I see no great value in my proving the absurdity of a position the proponents of which already grant its absurdity. The most consistent act of irrational philosophers would be simply to shut up. If they can say nothing meaningful (since there is nothing meaningful to say), why continue babbling? They insist, however, on speaking and writing. In a word, they argue for the "truth" of their position, but their arguments have no grounds for validity or invalidity since they have already abandoned the law of validity.

When I challenge such pseudo-philosophers in this manner, they reply that they have no need to be consistent or rational because reality and truth are neither consistent nor rational. Indeed, this would be a "rational" defense of irrationality. But to seek to justify irrationality by rational means begs the question in piercing screams. It is self-defeating, because it employs the very norms it is attacking. It is the classic case of wanting to eat one's cake and have it too.

To claim irrationality allows a thinker to be as sloppy as he wishes without making himself vulnerable to a sober critique. If we point out inconsistency, contradiction, or error, he can respond, "See, I told you my position is absurd."

One wonders what Zeno of Elea would do with such thinkers. His favorite ploy, the *reductio ad absurdum* argument, would be short-circuited. How does one reduce to absurdity something that is already absurd? What a monumental waste of time! When I debate someone who claims irrationality at the outset, I see no need to refute him; he has already done that for me. I hand back the microphone and ask him politely to state his position again, but more loudly. If he declares that his alternative to theism is absurd, he has done all I can hope to achieve in my arguments for theism. The only tactic I have left is that of ridicule. We should laugh (albeit through tears) at those views that are declared by their proponents to be absurd.

The irony, however, is that most proponents of absurdity take umbrage at being deemed absurd proponents of absurdity. They want to be regarded as cogent defenders of absurdity, which is a fool's errand. For if Nietzsche's (or anyone else's) argument for irrationality is true, then it must be false!

The apostle Paul declares that God has clearly manifested himself to all men, so that everyone knows his eternal power and deity and is without excuse when failing to honor him as God. As a consequence of this refusal to acknowledge what they know to be true, they "became futile in their thoughts, and their foolish hearts were darkened." Paul continues, "Professing to be wise, they became fools" (Rom. 1:21-22). This apostolic testimony speaks to one of the vexing questions in the history of theoretical thought: How can brilliant scholars such as Aquinas and Nietzsche come to such radically opposing worldviews? If the spectrum of philosophical views ranges between full-orbed theism on one side and nihilism on the other, how can men of genius end up so far apart?

Perhaps the answer lies in this: If at the earliest stages of intellectual reflection a person denies the existence of God, then the

Figure 12.1
Spectrum of Philosophical Views

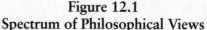

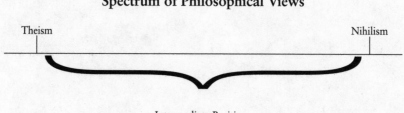

Intermediate Positions
(e.g., hybrid humanism)

more brilliant he is, the farther his thought will move away from God. Most secular philosophers end up somewhere between the two poles, living on borrowed capital from either theism or nihilism. Without God, nihilism, as nonsensical as it is, makes more sense than a hybrid humanism or any other intermediate position.

Although I do not embrace presuppositional apologetics, I do recognize that the existence of God is the supreme *proto*-supposition for all theoretical thought. God's existence is the chief element in constructing any worldview. To deny this chief premise is to set one's sails for the island of nihilism. This is the darkest continent of the darkened mind—the ultimate paradise of the fool.

13

Jean-Paul Sartre:
Litterateur and Philosopher

During the second half of the twentieth century, philosophy was dominated by existential (or phenomenological) philosophy on the one hand and by analytical philosophy on the other. From the phenomenological side the two dominant thinkers were Martin Heidegger and Jean-Paul Sartre.

Rarely in the history of thought have dominant thinkers emerged from a common source. One example is the ancient triumvirate of Socrates, Plato, and Aristotle, whose work has eclipsed all other such schools in importance. In the past century, however, we have witnessed another triumvirate that rivals but does not equal the Socratic school: Edmund Husserl, Martin Heidegger, and Jean-Paul Sartre. These three are tied together by a common thread, one that begins with Husserl.

Edmund Husserl

Edmund Husserl (1859–1938) is generally recognized as the father of modern phenomenology. After studying under Franz Brentano, Husserl taught first at the University of Halle, then at the University of Göttingen. In 1916 he moved to the University of Freiburg, where he taught until 1928. Because he was Jewish, he was forbidden to participate in Germany's academic life after 1933.

Acknowledging a debt to Descartes, Husserl makes self-consciousness the starting point of his philosophical reflection. The essence of human personality resides in what he calls intentionality. He argues that one's immediate knowledge of one's own mental state is the only sure foundation for understanding. One must, however, isolate what is intrinsic to the mental state and distinguish it from all that is extraneous to it. The "intentionality" of the mental makes meaning essential to every mental act.

For Husserl, however, the bare fact of consciousness is not the clearest truth of human experience; consciousness is always a consciousness of *something*. This consciousness of things the mind must intentionally "bracket." This bracketing is a kind of detachment from any objective point of view. Husserl refuses to assert whether or not the world exists. "For me," he says, "the world is nothing other than what I am aware of and what appears valid in my acts of thought."

For Husserl the world derives its meaning from the self's experience of phenomena. Husserl limits the scope of philosophy to the phenomenal experience. The world is as my consciousness intends it to be. Our understanding of things determines the essence of things; the essence of things does not determine our understanding. Here we see the root of the existential credo, "Existence precedes essence."

Martin Heidegger

Martin Heidegger (1889–1976), a student of Husserl, became his assistant at Freiburg in 1920 and succeeded him in 1927. Heidegger is often lumped together with existential philosophers despite his disclaimer that he was not an existentialist. His chief concern was to construct a new ontology or theory of being. Heidegger's *magnum opus* was entitled *Being and Time (Sein und Zeit*).[1] In the early years of the Third Reich, Heidegger supported the Nazis. He later became disillusioned with them but because of his earlier affiliation was forbidden to teach in Germany after the war.

Heidegger's starting point for ontology is man. He defines man with the term *Dasein,* which means literally "being there." Man is not a thing; he is a being, but his "being" is always in the world. It is not an abstraction but a being "there." Man begins by finding himself in a state of what Heidegger calls "thrownness." Man finds himself hurled, as it were, passively, into his peculiar existence. He is thrown into the midst of life, and he is responsible to take the initiative in discovering the meaning of his existence. He hangs precariously in a kind of Kierkegaardian either/or situation. He can either interpret himself as a thing—one thing among others—or he can make his possibilities the reason for his existence. The choice is between inauthentic and authentic existence.

The "inauthentic" man makes uncritical assumptions, and his thoughts are preoccupied with everyday concerns. His joy is always at the mercy of what happens externally. In a sense the newspaper or television does his thinking for him. His thought-life is merely an exercise in distraction to avoid restlessness or boredom, a kind of continual woolgathering.

Another way to describe inauthentic existence is that it is absorbed in the mere passing of time. Life is reduced to a mere pastime. Indeed, it is the element of time that presses the issue. The time element is critical to our experience of thrownness. Heidegger says we know time because we know we will die. *Tempus fugit* is a stark reality that engulfs us in temporal existence. Every moment of our lives we are in fact running out of time. Because we ever find ourselves in the here and now *(hic et nunc),* our fundamental mood is that of angst or "anxiety."

Like Sigmund Freud, Heidegger distinguishes between fear and anxiety. Fear is directed toward a specific object: a dog, a snake, a boss, a mortgage payment, or another external reality that threatens us. Anxiety is far worse and much more unsettling. It is amorphous. We cannot name its object, yet it hangs like the sword of Damocles over our lives. One can flee from the object of fear, but escape from anxiety is more difficult. The inauthentic man, when he runs from his fears, takes his anxiety with him.

The authentic man says no to all forms of escapism. He meets his anxiety head-on. The authentic man realizes that anxiety can be both destructive and constructive. It can cause flight into inauthenticity, or it can be the catalyst for freedom. Man becomes authentic by making the right decisions.

The inauthentic person seeks safety in normality. He denies his uniqueness by becoming "average." In this respect he acts much like a member of Friedrich Nietzsche's "herd." He believes as he is expected to believe, in accordance with societal convention. Suppressing the urge to excel, he levels himself downward and becomes "everyman." He abandons responsibility for his decisions and hence for his existence. He surrenders his ego and adopts the viewpoint of a victim. But still he does not escape anxiety, an inescapable mode of man's being. Anxiety, we recall, has no object. It is no thing, or more precisely "nothing." Anxiety manifests the threat of "nothingness" (the *nihil*) in our being. It is inevitable that we will die.

The authentic man comes to grips with the threat of nothingness. He knows he cannot escape his limitations, chiefly his temporality and finitude. Man conquers this through sheer resolve. He seeks to realize his potential in fullest measure. He faces the nothingness at every moment, living, as it were, in advance of himself. He faces the future by taking full responsibility for his past. He decides to accept the past and confront his destiny with intentionality.

This brings to mind the death of Ernest Hemingway. Hemingway acknowledged that he could not defeat death. The only victory he could achieve over death was to decide for himself the manner and moment of his death. One evening after his wife retired, he meticulously set up his favorite hunting rifle so that by simply pulling the trigger he could blow out his brains.

Jean-Paul Sartre

Jean-Paul Sartre (1905–1980) studied first in Paris and later in Germany, where he heard Husserl lecture and studied with Heidegger. Sartre's first novel, *Nausea*,[2] is a commentary on the human predicament. This work, which Sartre considered his best, established him as an author of extraordinary talent.

During World War II Sartre became active in the French Resistance, for which the Germans made him a prisoner of war. While in prison he continued to study and expound on Heidegger's philosophy. He was also heavily influenced by Marxism, but he never joined the Communist Party. When he won the Nobel Prize for literature, he refused to accept the award on the grounds that it would turn him into an institution.

In his student days Sartre met his lifelong companion, Simone de Beauvoir, who became France's most celebrated writer.

Sartre's literary output includes plays such as *The Flies* and *No Exit*.[3] His most prodigious philosophical work was *Being and Nothingness*,[4] published in 1943.

Sartre is known for his dictum, "Existence precedes essence." This concept is directly linked to his atheism. Previous atheists, after denying God's existence, still tended to speak of human "nature." The term *human nature* assumes an "essence" common to all humanity; but to have an essence, according to Sartre, one would have to be more like a thing than a person. Sartre makes a contrast between manufactured things and human beings. The former are designed and made to fit the function or purpose conceived by their maker. The idea of the thing, its essence, precedes its manufacture, which creates its actual existence. In the case of manufactured objects, their essence precedes their existence. For the same thing to be true of human beings, there would have to be a maker who designs and creates them. The creator would have an idea of what he intends to make and would have in mind a purpose for his creation.

Since Sartre believes there is no God, he believes there is no prior idea for human beings, no design or purpose for them. There is no human essence or nature to which individual humans correspond or conform.

In the case of man, says Sartre, existence precedes essence. Man simply is. He exists and only later defines himself. Man is or becomes whatever he makes of himself. This is not to say that man is self-created; he is not created at all—he simply is, and he must define himself. In this sense man "creates" whatever he becomes, but he does not bring himself into existence. He creates himself in a different way, by creating his own values.

Sartre distinguishes between *l'en-soi* (being-in-itself) and *le pour-soi* (being-for-itself). For Sartre, human consciousness is not a "thing." Knowledge is not a relationship between one thing (a mind) and another thing (objects in the physical world). Consciousness is always an awareness of something, but at the same time it is an awareness of itself as not being a thing. Epistemologically we should start not with "I am conscious of myself," but with "I am a consciousness."

L'en soi, being-in-itself, is simply there. In Sartre's novel *Nausea*, the protagonist, Roquentin, faces the stark "thereness" of the root of a chestnut tree. He reflects on the root, analyzing how it can be used by man. He peels away its meaning until he reaches a sense of radical absurdity, which arouses in him the feeling of nausea. Like the roots of the chestnut tree, the phenomenal being of every object is just "there." All things are simply superfluous. Everything is contingent and there is no reason for anything. All things share equally in meaninglessness. To exist is simply to be there as an obscene fact.

The only difference between man and beings-in-themselves is that man is also *pour-soi,* a conscious subject. This conscious subjectivity makes us different from rocks and roots. It makes us responsible for our own existence. Rocks and roots cannot be responsible.

Freedom and Responsibility

For Sartre it is not so much that man *has* freedom as that human existence *is* freedom. His notion of freedom encompasses the idea of moral autonomy. Man is not subject to objective rules. No norms govern his behavior. Sartre insists on such autonomy as a consequence of his atheism. Like Heidegger, Sartre speaks of the human sense of being *abandoned* in the universe. Out of the resulting anxiety man is, as it were, "forced" to be free. Man must choose for himself what he will become.

Man is in the situation Sartre describes in his play *The Flies,* patterned after the tale of Clytemnestra's murder of her husband Agamemnon and the plan of their son Orestes to kill Clytemnestra to avenge his father. Finding himself abandoned, Orestes murders his mother not so much to avenge his father as to give substance to his own life. ". . . there was nothing left in heaven, no right or wrong, nor anyone to give me orders. . . . For I . . . am a man, and every man must find out his own way."[5]

For Sartre, freedom is freedom from morality. Freedom must embrace what is disgusting. At one point Sartre describes man as a "useless passion." This description identifies two distinct aspects of human existence. First, man is a being who feels and cares. He has passion. We normally associate passion with some goal (we have a passion *for* something), but (second) man's passion is "useless." It is futile and meaningless. And the more I consider my cares and feelings to be futile, the greater my sense of futility.

This futility fuels the anxiety that is connected to freedom. Freedom is a given of my existence. I "must" be free; I am not free to not be free. Freedom is a burden that can crush the human spirit.

While in seminary I was walking through the East Liberty section of Pittsburgh on a Saturday evening. As I passed a jewelry store, a man ran out the door and collided with me. I grabbed him so that neither of us would fall to the ground. As I held him in my grasp, he looked me in the eye and meekly said, "I surrender." At that moment a woman ran out of the store shouting, "Stop! Thief!" The man, unarmed, had just robbed the jewelry store. While he waited calmly, the police arrived to take him into custody. The following day I met one of the arresting officers and asked him about the man I had "captured." The officer explained that the robber had been released from jail the previous day and had not wanted to leave. He committed a new crime, making sure that he was "captured," so that he could return to the safety and security of his jail cell. In jail he had three meals a day and a bed to sleep in. This was a man who could not dare to be free. The anxiety that attends freedom was too much for him. He was the quintessential "inauthentic man."

The anxiety of freedom, according to Sartre, is exacerbated by the fact that a person must move forward with no assurance that he is on the right track. He can never be sure that he is on the right track, because in the final analysis there is no right track.

When Alice, walking in Wonderland, comes to a fork in the road, she does not know which way to go. She sees the Cheshire Cat smiling at her from its perch in a tree. Alice asks the cat, "Would you tell me, please, which way I ought to go from here?"

"That depends a good deal on where you want to get to," says the cat.

"I don't much care where—" says Alice.

"Then it doesn't matter which way you go," says the cat.[6]

This is but a small step removed from the sagacious advice of the great American philosopher Yogi Berra: "If you come to a fork in the road, take it."

What price freedom? Man, with no support and aid, is condemned every moment to invent man. Similar to Immanuel Kant's "golden rule" of the categorical imperative is Sartre's principle: When a man makes a choice or decision, he acts not only for himself but also for all men. He is responsible not only for his own individuality but also for all mankind.

This seems to, and probably does, contradict everything else Sartre says about existence. Now the individual is given the responsibility, and therefore the ability, to determine not only his essence but also the essence of everyone else. But this robs everyone else of the freedom to create their own essences. At this point the choosing individual acts very much like God, who by his will imposes essence on others.

Freedom and God

Sartre declares that he is not happy with his conclusion that God does not exist. He says he does not enjoy the prospect of facing life without divine support. He criticizes sharply philosophers who, while denying God's existence, argue for essential norms of truth, honesty, justice, goodness, and so forth. He takes seriously Fyodor Dostoyevsky's dictum, "If God does not exist, all things are permissible."

Sartre has several arguments against the existence of God that rest primarily on his conviction that man is a free subject rather than merely an object. Like others before him, Sartre maintains that the idea of God is the product of man's creative consciousness. Religious belief is not rooted in communion with God or communication from God. Rather, it is merely a wish projection. It flows from one's fearful reluctance to face constant threats from insecurity, frustration, and the specter of meaninglessness. Every fiber of man's life screams in protest against the thought of nihilism. Those who cannot take it create a god to help them cope.

Sartre argues that God's existence and man's freedom are mutually exclusive categories. If God exists, man cannot be free. That is, if God creates man's essence and governs his existence, man cannot really be free. Freedom is not true freedom unless it is absolute. Anything less than autonomy is not true freedom. The idea of "limited freedom" is contradictory.

Sartre's protest is not unlike the serpent's in the Garden of Eden. In Genesis the serpent is described as "more cunning [or subtle] than any beast of the field" (Gen. 3:1). He approaches Eve with the provocative question, "Has God indeed said, 'You shall not eat of every tree of the garden'?" (Gen. 3:1). The serpent knows well that God has given Adam and Eve a measure of freedom. Indeed, God had said to them, "Of every tree of the garden you may freely eat" (Gen. 2:16). Then he added one restriction: "But of the tree of the knowledge of good and evil you shall not eat, for in the day that you eat of it you shall surely die" (Gen. 2:17).

The cunning question the serpent uses to seduce Eve suggests that, if there is one restriction, one limit imposed on human freedom, then man is not truly free. It is like the child who, after receiving ten "yesses" from his parents, receives one "no" and then protests, "You never let me do anything!"

Sartre is right: Human autonomy is incompatible with the idea of God. But the question remains: Must a person be completely autonomous in order to be free?

One of Sartre's most fascinating and unique arguments against the existence of God has to do with man's subjectivity. Remember the chief premise of Sartre's existential philosophy: Man is a subject, not an object. Sartre believes that this subjectivity would be destroyed if there were a God. In *Being and Nothingness* Sartre devotes a section to what he calls "the Look."[7] He describes what happens when people are subjected to the gaze of others. Beneath another person's stare I am reduced to the status of an object. It is appropriate for people to stare for protracted periods at paintings in a museum, or at monkeys in a zoo. But it is not acceptable for people to stare at each other or to maintain eye contact beyond a couple of seconds while passing on the street. We interpret a stare as a hostile act.

Sartre muses about sitting at a table in a café on the Left Bank of Paris and feeling someone's gaze upon his back. (Due to his fame he undoubtedly had to endure the rudeness of people whispering about him and rubber-necking to see him in public places.) This reduction to an object creates what he calls "existential self-awareness" and the destruction of subjectivity.

No Exit

Sartre develops this theme in his play *No Exit*. The protagonist, Garcin, finds himself in a room with two other people. Near the end of the play, Garcin speaks:

"This bronze. *[Strokes it thoughtfully.]* Yes, now's the moment; I'm looking at this thing on the mantelpiece, and I understand that I'm in hell. I tell you, everything's been thought out beforehand. They knew I'd stand at the fireplace stroking this thing of bronze, with all those eyes intent on me. Devouring me. *[He swings around abruptly.]* What? Only two of you? I thought there were more; many more. *[Laughs.]* So this is hell. I'd never have believed it. You remember all we were told about the torture-chambers, the fire and brimstone, the 'burning marl.' Old wives' tales! There's no need for red-hot pokers. Hell is—other people!"[8]

The final stage direction in the play reads: "They slump into their respective sofas. A long silence. Their laughter dies away and they gaze at each other."[9]

If the gaze of other people destroys our subjectivity, Sartre wonders, how much worse would it be to be constantly under the gaze of God? Sartre sees omniscience turning God into a cosmic voyeur whose gaze reduces all men to objects. God peers through a celestial keyhole like a malevolent peeping Tom, ever destroying human subjectivity. But since man is really a subject, there can be no God. Beneath God's eternal gaze we would all become objects, essences rather than existences.

Scripture frequently records the discomfort of the guilty who seek shelter from God's sight, calling on the hills to cover them. Sinful man does not want God to look at him; he wants God to *overlook* him. Yet from a biblical perspective the forgiven sinner knows no blessing equal to God's benevolent gaze; he enjoys the light of God's countenance upon him and wants God to make his face shine upon him.

According to Dutch philosopher Wilhelmus Luijpen, Sartre insists that morality makes the existence of God impossible, but in truth Sartre's morality makes the denial of God's existence necessary.

Table 13.1
Eight Men Who Changed the World

	Birth–death	Nationality	Position
René Descartes	1596–1650	French	
John Locke	1632–1704	English	Commissioner of Appeal (1689–1704)
David Hume	1711–1776	Scottish	Director, law library, Edinburgh (1752–1763)
Immanuel Kant	1724–1804	German	Professor, Königsberg (1755–1797)
Karl Marx	1818–1883	German	Leader, International Workingmen's Assoc., London (from 1864)
Søren Kierkegaard	1813–1855	Danish	
Friedrich Nietzsche	1844–1900	German	Professor of philology, Basel (1869–1879)
Jean-Paul Sartre	1905–1980	French	Teacher in LaHavre, Laon, Paris (1931–1945)

Darwin and Freud: Influential Thinkers

Our chief focus has been on philosophers whose ideas have had a major impact on Western culture. We have noticed that many of these philosophers were also engaged in the academic pursuit of science and mathematics. From Thales to Plato, Aristotle, René Descartes, Immanuel Kant, and others, a common thread of concern has been the relationship of philosophical inquiry to scientific theory.

Though neither Charles Darwin nor Sigmund Freud is usually classified as a philosopher, both men published theories that had a profound effect on Western theoretical thought. The publication of Darwin's *The Origin of Species*[1] was as revolutionary as the publication of Copernicus's *On the Revolution of Heavenly Spheres*.

Yet as revolutionary as the shift from geocentricity to heliocentricity was, it pales in comparison with the impact of Darwin's ideas. His name has become synonymous with the word *evolution*, though theories of evolution predated his work and though there is no single, monolithic "theory" of evolution but multiple theories with various nuances. That is, the idea of evolution has itself evolved and undergone various changes, but Darwin's name remains central to this development.

It is natural to expect a link to emerge between natural science and history. History deals not only with the activities of human beings over time but also with the setting for these activities in the realm of nature. One's understanding of the universe's origin (cosmogony), nature (cosmology), and age has a profound impact on one's anthropology and theology. In these two fields Darwin's work provoked the greatest crisis.

Darwin and Theology

The issue of human origins becomes one of fierce emotions, fueling the Scopes trial and more recent controversies over teaching creation in public schools. If the Copernican revolution created a rift between science and religion, the Darwinian revolution expanded this rift into an unbridgeable canyon.

At stake in the controversy, in the first instance, is the dignity of human beings. If, as some contend, human beings emerged not due to divine intelligence and action but due to impersonal forces of nature, the question of human dignity becomes acute. Man's present dignity is inseparably bound up with his past and future, with his origin and destiny.

As we have seen in various forms of nihilism and pessimistic existentialism, the issue of origin is critical. One philosopher mused that man is but a grown-up germ. He emerged fortuitously from the slime and sits precariously on the rim of one cog of one gear of a vast cosmic machine that is destined for annihilation. If indeed we came from the abyss of non-being and are being hurled relentlessly back to this abyss, what value, worth, or dignity do we have? If our origin and destiny are meaningless, how can our lives now have any meaning? To assign dignity to such a cosmic accident, who is at best bestial, is to succumb to maudlin forms of wish-projection and philosophical naiveté. This was clearly understood by Friedrich Nietzsche, Jean-Paul Sartre, and others.

Radical evolution has the salutary appeal to some of eliminating the threat of a supreme Judge before whose judgment they will be held accountable for their lives and behavior. If radical evolutionary theory is correct, then one has nothing to fear from such a judge. Grown-up germs are not morally accountable in any ultimate way. The price tag for this escape from accountability, however, is Sartre's "useless passion." Simply stated, if we are not ultimately accountable for our lives, then our lives do not and cannot count ultimately.

In 1831 Charles Darwin set sail for an around-the-world voyage to make scientific observations and do empirical research. He took along Charles Lyell's book *Principles of Geology*,[2] a lucid defense of uniformitarian geology. Uniformitarianism argues strenuously against theories of catastrophism, which raised the serious issue of the earth's age. Uniformitarian geology requires an earth millions of years old to account for profound changes in rock and soil, the raising and lowering of mountains, and so forth.

Darwin rhapsodizes about Lyell's book and its influence on his thinking. While near Tahiti, well into his voyage, Darwin worked out his theory of the formation of coral atolls. Darwin convincingly argues that since living coral requires sunlight and cannot live at a depth greater than 100 feet, the formation of layers of coral into an atoll must take time and cannot, even through catastrophic upheaval, be instantaneous.

In 1859 Darwin published *The Origin of Species*. He had begun it in 1839 and had basically finished it by 1844. He withheld it from publication for fifteen years, probably fearful of the outrage it might provoke. In the book he theorizes that all living organisms on earth have descended from a single primordial form. From that single source all varieties of life have evolved and continue to evolve. This is the essence of *macroevolution*. This dif-

fers from *microevolution,* which restricts evolution to changes and
adaptations within a group.

Darwin's Major Premises

Timothy Ferris, in *Coming of Age in the Milky Way,* cites the three
major premises of Darwin's theory:

*Premise 1: Each individual member of a given species is dif-
ferent.* The uniqueness of the individual is certainly affirmed today
for the species *Homo sapiens.* In modern times individual dis-
tinctives are linked to the genetic code. To prove an individual's
identity, forensic pathology now prefers DNA over such techniques as fingerprinting.

In nineteenth-century England, great interest had developed in
animal husbandry and plant hybridization. Darwin's father-in-law
was an animal breeder interested in how individual characteristics
could be bred into the next generation. Darwin's grandfather,
Erasmus Darwin, wrote a book titled *Zoonomia*[3] *(The Laws of
Organic Life),* in which he argues that all life could have evolved
from a common ancestor.

*Premise 2: All living creatures tend to produce more offspring
than the environment can support.* This leads some to see in
nature (or in God) a certain wastefulness or crudity. Only a percentage of newborn insects, animals, fish, and so forth live long
enough to reproduce. Even in human reproduction, though the
egg of the female is fertilized by only one sperm, a single male ejaculation may contain millions of sperm. Why the waste? (A more
sanguine way to see this picture is in terms not of waste but of
assurance. If 999,999 sperm are "wasted" to assure the fertiliza-
tion of one egg, this indicates a powerful drive toward species
survival and continuity.) This leads Darwin to his third premise,
which involves the process of "natural selection."

Premise 3: Differences among individuals, combined with environmental pressures, affect the probability that a given individual will survive long enough to pass along its genetic traits.

An example is the peppered moths near Manchester, England. Throughout the eighteenth century all moths collected in the region were pallid in color. In 1849 a single black moth was caught. By 1880 the black moths were the majority. Why? What changed the balance of moths? Darwin looks not to some inherent strength or weakness of the moths, but to changes of environmental processes. In Manchester the industrial revolution represented an outside force that changed the moth's environment. Soot from factories blackened tree trunks, robbing the original moths of the benefits of camouflage and decreasing their numbers. Darker trees bestowed a singular camouflage on the few black moths, however, so they proliferated. When antipollution laws went into effect, the soot slowly washed off of the trees and the pale-moth population rebounded.[4]

Darwin and Macroevolution

From these basic premises, which had the benefit of empirical corroboration, a much more complex and far-reaching theory could develop. Darwin concludes that natural selection not only prompts changes within species but leads to the origination of new species. Macroevolution requires that new species evolve from different species. This is what has provoked such controversy and has raised the specter of humans descending from brutish beasts.

Some maintain that macroevolution can no longer be called a theory or hypothesis but should be regarded as incontrovertible fact. This reflects the almost religious zeal accompanying the current theories, which rivals in intensity the religious zeal that opposes them.

Much remains, however, for evolutionary theory to establish. The origin of biological species, in the final analysis, is not so much a biological as a historical question. That organisms in this world evidence change is nothing new. It was evident to Thales and was an article of truth for Heraclitus. The question of how becoming relates to being is as old as philosophy. How and why becoming moves has been for philosophers a perennial concern.

We frequently hear that our modern understanding of the nature of living organisms proves macroevolution. As the argument goes, the fact that all living things are composed of the same basic substance or "stuff," such as amino acids, proteins, and so forth, proves that all life came from the same source. But to conclude common source from the premise of common substance is fallacious reasoning. Common substance no more requires a common source than the occurrence of one thing after another proves that the first caused the second (the *post hoc* fallacy).

Evolutionary theories usually assume that all changes involved in mutations, natural selection, and so forth are part of an upward spiral of progress. Such "progress" suggests a goal or a purpose. But this involves an assumption of teleology or design. Design without a designer, like aim without an aimer, begs the question of intelligence.

Why do not such theories of change assume that the changes are devolutionary or regressive? Why not simply deem these changes meaningless? When examining these questions, we see quickly that in the final analysis evolution is a question not so much of biology as of philosophy.

Freud on Culture and Religion

Another thinker who, though not a philosopher, has had a massive influence on modern culture is Sigmund Freud. Generally considered the founder of psychoanalysis, Freud was born in Austria in 1856. He received his M.D. in 1881 in Vienna. In 1885 he studied neurology in Paris with Jean Martin Charcot. When the Nazis came to power, Freud fled to England, where he died in 1939.

Though noted in the field of psychology, Freud was also keenly interested in anthropology. In 1913 he wrote *Totem and Taboo*,[5] in which he explores the origin of totemic religion. After 1923 Freud turned more and more to the study of culture. Two of his most important works from this period are *The Future of an Illusion* (1927) and *Civilization and Its Discontents* (1929).[6]

In his analysis of culture, Freud's chief hypothesis is that every individual person is an enemy of civilization. Though individuals can barely exist in isolation from other people, they nevertheless find the personal sacrifices that make civilization and community life possible to be a weighty burden.

Civilization, says Freud, is imposed on the majority by a controlling or coercive minority. Coercion is necessary because of two basic human characteristics: 1) Men are not spontaneously fond of work, and 2) human passions often overrule reason.

Cultures tend to exalt their leaders and view their own customs as superior to those of other cultures. Within a culture the favored classes enjoy a narcissistic satisfaction with their status. But the suppressed classes are also satisfied because they can still look down on people who are outside of and "beneath" their culture.

Perhaps the strongest element of culture and civilization is religion, which contributes to the internalization of cultural taboos.

At this point Freud attempts to account for religion's origin. In the late nineteenth and early twentieth centuries atheism turned its attention to a vexing question: If God does not exist, why do human beings appear to be *Homo Religiosus*—religious beings? Wherever societies are found, they manifest elements of religion.

An incredible penchant for religious belief seems to be inherent in humanity.

The most common explanation for the widespread phenomenon of religion is that it is rooted in a deep psychological need or wish-projection. We recall Karl Marx's conclusion that the bourgeoisie uses religion to control the proletariat. Religion is the opium with which the workers are drugged and made docile. The African slave in America was encouraged to sing "Swing Low, Sweet Chariot." He was promised a blissful paradise in the afterlife, where he would be free and happy, but to obtain that reward he must be docile and obedient in this life.

Though similar theories were posed by Feuerbach and Nietzsche, Freud explored the psychology of the religious impulse most fully. Freud concludes that the chief task, the *raison d'etre*, of civilization is to protect and defend us against nature. Nature manifests elements that seem to mock human control. Earthquakes tear apart and bury human life and structures. Floods destroy everything in their path and drown people. Dreadful diseases inflict suffering and pain. Then there is the big enemy, what Freud calls the "painful riddle of death," for which no medicine has been discovered.

To create a defense against the forces of nature, says Freud, one must personalize them. Impersonal powers are remote; they cannot be approached safely. How does one persuade a hurricane to stop blowing? Who can negotiate with cancer? How can we ever appeal to an earthquake or reason with a flood?

We do have experience dealing with *people* who threaten us. With them, we have several options: become obsequious and submit to their authority; befriend them and appeal to their egos by fawning over them with praise; appeal to their compassion by begging for mercy; or appease them by offering expensive gifts or bribes.

The first step, then, in escaping nature's threats is to humanize and *personalize* nature. If we give passions to the elements, passions like ours, we can defend ourselves from them effectively.

The second step is to *sacralize* nature. The personalized powers of nature become objects of religious devotion. In evolutionary terms, the process moves from the simple to the complex. Like organisms, religion begins simply and then progresses to more complex forms.

In the nineteenth century many scholars thought that religion progresses from animism to polytheism (there are many gods) to henotheism (there are many gods but one is supreme) to monotheism (there is only one God). To Freud, animism represents the early stages of religious development. It is the simplest, most rudimentary religion. Animism takes inanimate objects such as rocks, trees, totem poles, and storms, and assigns to them indwelling, living spirits, thus "animating" them. Modern research into primitive tribes still practicing animism indicates that the spirits thought to inhabit these objects are almost always malevolent and almost never benevolent. These evil spirits must be appeased to avoid the evil they dispense.

Religion eventually develops into a complex monotheism that affirms a benevolent Providence. With this kindly Providence we have a filial relationship. God is now a single person whom we call Father and with whom we enjoy a childlike sense of intimacy and reliance.

Religion, says Freud, has a threefold task: 1) to exorcise the terrors of nature; 2) to reconcile us to the cruelty of fate; and 3) to compensate us for the sufferings and privations civilization has imposed.

One of the greatest privations imposed by civilization, according to Freud, is the loss of free sexual expression. Society imposes customs and laws that function as taboos. As a result, man's erotic life is dramatically mutilated. The sexually mature individual must restrict himself to the opposite sex. Extra-genital satisfactions are called perversions and forbidden. Civilization requires a single kind of sexual life, ignoring dissimilarities and cutting off many persons from sexual enjoyment. Civilization's insistence on monogamous sex is sanctioned by religion, which exacerbates the individual's sense of alienation. All of this, says Freud, becomes a source of serious injustice.

Freud essentially called for and predicted the sexual revolution, which he did not live to see.

Freud and Guilt

Also contributing to the development of religion is a guilt linked to the image of God as father. In *Totem and Taboo* and *Civilization and Its Discontents*, Freud sets forth the hypothesis of a primordial tribal struggle between the father-chief and his young sons. The struggle culminates in the sons murdering their father, an act that leaves the sons with tormented consciences that can be relieved only by deifying their father's image and worshiping him. Fear of nature combined with guilt toward a father comprise Freud's two-sided basis for religious belief and practice.

Freud's basic thesis is that people invent religion out of a fear of nature. To reduce this fear they personalize nature. Then they sacralize it, yet it never becomes personally holy. According to the Bible, there is something even more threatening, more traumatic, to the human psyche then the impersonal forces of nature. If nature is impersonal and non-holy, we need fear only its power. If God is both personal and holy, however, we must fear not only his power but also his judgment.

In biblical terms, the ultimate object of religion is salvation—rescue from the wrath of God. We are saved, not from the earthquake or storm, but from God. He is the most threatening reality we face because he is holy and we are not. (If we invent God merely to avert a threat from nature, why invent one who is infinitely more threatening than nature itself?)

Mark recounts an episode when Jesus was with his disciples in a boat on the Sea of Galilee (Mark 4:35-41). A fierce gale arises, causing monstrous waves to crash against the boat and threaten to capsize it. The disciples are afraid, but Jesus is in the back of the boat, sound asleep. The disciples awaken him and say, "Do You not care that we are perishing?"

Jesus stands up and shouts at the wind and the sea: "Peace, be still!" Instantly the winds stop raging. There is not even a zephyr in the air, and the lake's surface becomes like glass.

How do the disciples respond? They become exceedingly fearful. Their fear is magnified, growing more intense rather than less. What terrifies them now is Jesus. They cry out, "What manner of man is this?" (Mark 4:41, KJV). They are experiencing xenophobia—the fear of the stranger or alien. Nothing is more alien to them than one who can command the sea and the wind. They are in the presence of the supreme alien—the transcendent one— the Holy One of Israel—from whom men and devils flee the moment they recognize him.

Guilt causes people to flee. Freud's theory is a massive attempt to escape his own guilt. He understands that to escape guilt he must first escape God. So much of modern thought is an attempt to escape the one who is inescapable.

CONCLUSION:

Gilson's Choice

During the transition into the twenty-first century, the realm of theoretical thought remains in crisis. As in previous periods of skepticism, the world awaits the rescue of metaphysics by a new synthesis that will overcome the agnostic philosophy of Immanuel Kant. Like the children of ancient Israel, we stand between Migdol and the sea. Behind us are the chariots of Pharaoh's army; in front is the seemingly impassable Red Sea. We need a Moses who will raise his arms, and we need God to provide us dry passage across the sea.

In this volume we have provided a brief introductory sketch of the leading voices in the history of Western thought. I have been selective, and one can reasonably argue that some philosophers I have omitted should have been included, and some I have included should have been omitted.

For example, I have not included John Dewey (1859–1952), who along with Charles Peirce, William James, and others was a chief architect of pragmatism, America's only homegrown philosophical movement. In his widely distributed book *The Secular City*,[1] Harvard University's Harvey Cox sees pragmatism as defining the very shape of American culture. Pragmatism cut the Gordian knot of metaphysics by arguing that a theory is true only insofar as its actions are "successful."

The Triumph of Pragmatism

In carrying out pragmatism's program, John Dewey succeeded in revolutionizing our public school system. He disparages episte-mology, considering it a pseudo-problem and a waste of time. He repudiates both the "innate" ideas of René Descartes and the blank tablet of John Locke. He denies that such issues are even a problem. Dewey's penchant for anti-intellectualism has con-tributed greatly to the mindlessness of public education. In his book *The Closing of the American Mind*, Allan Bloom chroni-cles the modern resistance to objective truth and the university's courtship with relativism.[2] We wonder why Johnny cannot read, write, think, and pray. What can we expect from a school system that eschews matters of epistemology from the outset? Gone is the classical method of education that produced the intellectual giants of the past—the trivium of grammar, logic, and rhetoric that pro-vided the foundation for the quadrivium of higher education. This was noted in the 1940s by Dorothy Sayers in *The Lost Tools of Learning*.[3]

No wonder that more than 2 million families in America are now engaged in the arduous task of homeschooling, or that there is a mass exodus from public schools to private schools (and a clamor for a school voucher system). Following the publication of Douglas Wilson's book *Recovering the Lost Tools of Learning: An Approach to Distinctively Christian Education*,[4] a network of Christian classical schools has been established.

My personal baptism into the public education crisis occurred in the 1960s when we sent our firstborn, our daughter, off to first grade. We enrolled her in a highly acclaimed "progressive" school in a Boston suburb. When she came home from school each day, I asked her what she had done. She murmured the nonresponsive answer children typically give. After a few weeks the school hosted a parents' night in which the principal would explain the school's philosophy of education. I attended eagerly.

The principal reviewed a typical daily schedule. He was both winsome and articulate. "If your children come home and tell you that they do jigsaw puzzles in class, don't be alarmed," he said. "They are not just 'playing.' From 9:00 A.M. to 9:17, they assemble these puzzles, which have been designed by pediatric neurosurgeons to develop the motor muscles of the fingers on the left hand." Then he went through each segment of the school day, demonstrating that every moment was spent in purposeful activity. This *tour de force* overwhelmed the audience with its detailed and erudite explanation of every element in the curriculum.

When finished he asked, "Are there any questions?" Spontaneous laughter erupted. Only a fool would raise a question after the principal had so masterfully covered all the bases.

I risked everyone's disdain by raising my hand. When the principal called on me, I said: "Sir, I am profoundly impressed by your careful analysis. You have made it clear that you do everything for a purpose. But there are only so many minutes in a day, and therefore you must be selective in choosing what specific purposes you want to achieve. My question is, Why did you select the particular purposes you have chosen? What is the ultimate purpose you use to decide which particular purposes you select? In other words, what kind of child are you trying to produce and why?"

The principal's face turned ashen, then beet-red. Without rancor and with humility, he replied: "I don't know. Nobody has ever asked me that question."

"Sir," I responded, "I deeply appreciate your candor and your spirit, but frankly, your answer terrifies me."

What I heard in this public forum was pragmatism with a

vengeance. There were purposes without purpose, truths without truth. There was no norm to determine what is ultimately pragmatic. I thought of Jesus' words, "What profit is it to a man if he gains the whole world, and loses his own soul?" (Matt. 16:26). Jesus was being practical. He was saying that every practical goal of proximate success sooner or later must be measured against an ultimate norm for its ultimate practical result.

We have also passed over logical positivism and linguistic analysis, which have also played leading roles in the twentieth century. We witnessed the failure of logical positivism because its chief axiom, the law of verification, fell by its own weight. The law states that the only meaningful statements are those that can be verified empirically. As we have seen, however, the verification principle is itself incapable of being verified empirically, so it too is meaningless.

Logical positivism gave way to linguistic analysis. It seems that the only valuable task left for philosophy is to explore the meaning and function of language. Ludwig Wittgenstein's *Tractatus Logico-philosophicus* (1921)[5] was the watershed moment for this philosophical movement. Linguistic analysis has made a remarkable contribution to our understanding of the function of language—both technical language and ordinary language. But it squeezes the scope of theoretical thought into a tiny box that excludes the ultimate issues and questions asked by metaphysicians since antiquity. In one sense the rise of linguistic analysis, like the waving of white flags, signals philosophy's metaphysical surrender to defeat.

The Reconstruction of Metaphysics

Serious attempts to reconstruct metaphysics have been mounted by such thinkers as Henri-Louis Bergson and Alfred North

Whitehead. Process philosophy and its twin, process theology, in an attempt to address the classic problem of being and becoming, have posited a bipolar deity who contains both being *and* becoming within himself and oscillates between them.

Ideas, as we have seen, have consequences. Sometimes these consequences are radical and dramatic, as in the cases of Marxism and existentialism. Since the skepticism of Kant, we have been "waiting for Godot," suffocated by naturalism but refusing to open the door to a transcendent God.

Those dissatisfied with any form of naturalism have sought desperately to regain contact with the transcendent, employing means ranging from skeptical fideism with its leap of faith, to irrational mysticism, occultism, and New Age techniques. Etienne Gilson has defined the gods of modern philosophy as "mere byproducts born of the philosophical decomposition of the Christian living God."

According to Gilson our choice today is not between Immanuel Kant and René Descartes or between G. W. F. Hegel and Søren Kierkegaard. We must choose instead between Kant and Thomas Aquinas. Gilson insists that all other positions are mere halfway houses on the road to either absolute religious agnosticism or the natural theology of Christian metaphysics.

As I enter the twilight years of my life, I am convinced that Gilson is fundamentally right. We need to reconstruct the classical synthesis by which natural theology bridges the special revelation of Scripture and the general revelation of nature. Such a reconstruction could end the war between science and theology. The thinking person could embrace nature without embracing naturalism. All of life, in its unity and diversity, could be lived *coram Deo,* before the face of God, under his authority and to his glory.

NOTES

INTRODUCTION: WHY PHILOSOPHY?

1. Roger Scruton, *From Descartes to Wittgenstein: A Short History of Modern Philosophy* (Boston: Routledge & Kegan Paul, 1981); Gordon Clark, *Thales to Dewey: A History of Philosophy* (Boston: Houghton Mifflin, 1957); and Samuel Stumpf, *Socrates to Sartre: A History of Philosophy* (New York: McGraw-Hill, 1966).

CHAPTER 1: THE FIRST PHILOSOPHERS

1. Carl Sagan, *Cosmos* (New York: Random, 1980).

CHAPTER 2: PLATO: REALIST AND IDEALIST

1. Plato, *Dialogues,* eds. Eric H. Warmington and Philip Rouse, Mentor (New York: Penguin, 1956).

2. Plato, *The Republic,* trans. Robin Waterfield, Oxford World's Classics (New York: Oxford University Press, 1998).

3. Plato, *Phaedo,* trans. David Gallop, Oxford World's Classics (New York: Oxford University Press, 1999).

4. Plato, *Meno,* in *Protagoras and Meno,* trans. and ed. W. K. C. Guthrie, Penguin Classics (New York: Penguin, 1957).

CHAPTER 3: ARISTOTLE: *THE* PHILOSOPHER

1. Aristotle, *The Nicomachean Ethics,* trans. and ed. David Ross, rev. J. R. Ackrill and J. O. Urmson, Oxford World's Classics (New York: Oxford University Press, 1998).

2. Will Durant, *The Story of Philosophy: The Lives and Opinions of the Greater Philosophers* (New York: Simon and Schuster, 1926), 82. In support, Durant cites the following passages from Aristotle's works: *Metaphysics,* 12.8; *The Nicomachean Ethics,* 10.8.

CHAPTER 4: AUGUSTINE: DOCTOR OF GRACE

1. Samuel Stumpf, *Socrates to Sartre: A History of Philosophy* (New York: McGraw-Hill, 1966), 121.

2. Augustine, *Confessions,* trans. and ed. Henry Chadwick, Oxford World's Classics (New York: Oxford University Press, 1998); *The City of God,* ed. David Knowles, trans. Henry Bettenson, Penguin Classics (New York: Penguin, 1984).

Chapter 5: Thomas Aquinas: Angelic Doctor

1. Thomas Aquinas, *Summa Theologica,* 5 vols. (Allen, Tex.: Christian Classics, 1981).

2. See R. C. Sproul, *Not a Chance: The Myth of Chance in Modern Science and Cosmology* (Grand Rapids, Mich.: Baker, 1994).

Chapter 6: René Descartes: Father of Modern Rationalism

1. Ptolemy, *The Almagest,* trans. and ed. G. J. Toomer (New York: Springer-Verlag, 1984).

2. Nicolaus Copernicus, *On the Revolution of Heavenly Spheres,* trans. Charles G. Wallis, Great Minds Science Series (Amherst, N.Y.: Prometheus, 1995).

3. René Descartes, *Discourse on Method,* in *Discourse on Method and The Meditations,* trans. and ed. F. E. Sutcliffe, Penguin Classics (New York: Penguin, 1968).

4. René Descartes, *Rules for the Direction of the Mind,* extracts in *Discourse on Method and Related Writings,* trans. and ed. Desmond M. Clarke, Penguin Classics (New York: Penguin, 1999).

Chapter 7: John Locke: Father of Modern Empiricism

1. Voltaire, *Candide: or Optimism,* trans. John Butt, ed. E. V. Rieu, Penguin Classics (Baltimore: Penguin, 1947).

2. John Locke, *An Essay Concerning Human Understanding,* ed. Alexander Campbell Fraser, 2 vols. (New York: Dover, 1959).

3. John Locke, *Two Treatises of [Civil] Government,* ed. Peter Laslett, student ed., Cambridge Texts in the History of Political Thought, eds. Raymond Geuss and Quentin Skinner (Cambridge: Cambridge University Press, 1988).

Chapter 8: David Hume: Skeptic

1. David Hume, *A Treatise of Human Nature,* ed. Ernest C. Mossner, Penguin Classics (New York: Penguin, 1986).

2. David Hume, *Essays Moral and Political,* in *Essays Moral, Political, and Literary,* ed. Eugene F. Miller, rev. ed., Liberty Classics Series (Indianapolis: Liberty Fund, 1987).

3. David Hume, *An Enquiry Concerning Human Understanding,* Great Books in Philosophy (Amherst, N.Y.: Prometheus, 1988).

4. David Hume, *Dialogue Concerning Natural Religion,* ed. J. C. A. Gaskin, Oxford World's Classics (New York: Oxford University Press, 1998).

Chapter 9: Immanuel Kant: Revolutionary Philosopher

1. Immanuel Kant, *Critique of Pure Reason,* trans. J. M. Meiklejohn, Great Books in Philosophy (Amherst, N.Y.: Prometheus, 1990).

2. See R. C. Sproul, *Not a Chance: The Myth of Chance in Modern Science and Cosmology* (Grand Rapids, Mich.: Baker, 1994).

CHAPTER 11: SØREN KIERKEGAARD: DANISH GADFLY

1. Jean-Paul Sartre, *Being and Nothingness: An Essay on Phenomenological Ontology,* trans. Hazel E. Barnes (New York: Philosophical Library, 1956).

2. Jean-Paul Sartre, *No Exit,* in *"No Exit" and Three Other Plays,* trans. Stuart Gilbert (New York: New Directions, 1989).

3. Søren Kierkegaard, *Either/Or,* ed. and trans. Howard V. Hong and Edna H. Hong, 2 vols. (Princeton, N.J.: Princeton University Press, 1987).

4. Søren Kierkegaard, *Fear and Trembling,* trans. Alastair Hannay, Penguin Classics (New York: Penguin, 1986).

5. Ibid., 54.

6. Søren Kierkegaard, *Attack upon "Christendom,"* trans. and ed. Walter Lowrie (Princeton, N.J.: Princeton University Press, 1968).

7. Søren Kierkegaard, *Concluding Unscientific Postscript to "Philosophical Fragments,"* ed. and trans. Howard V. Hong and Edna H. Hong, vol. 1, *Text* (Princeton, N.J.: Princeton University, 1992).

8. Ibid., 203.

9. Emil Brunner, *Truth as Encounter,* 2d ed., Preacher's Library (London: SCM, 1964). The title of the German edition is *Wahrheit als Begegnung.*

CHAPTER 12: FRIEDRICH NIETZSCHE: ATHEISTIC EXISTENTIALIST

1. Friedrich Nietzsche, *Thus Spake Zarathustra,* trans. and ed. R. J. Hollingdale, Penguin Classics (New York: Penguin, 1961).

CHAPTER 13: JEAN-PAUL SARTRE: LITTERATEUR AND PHILOSOPHER

1. Martin Heidegger, *Being and Time: A Translation of "Sein und Zeit,"* trans. Joan Stambaugh, SUNY Series in Contemporary Continental Philosophy (Albany, N.Y.: State University of New York Press, 1996).

2. Jean-Paul Sartre, *Nausea,* trans. Lloyd Alexander (New York: New Directions), 1959.

3. Jean-Paul Sartre, *"No Exit" and Three Other Plays,* trans. Stuart Gilbert (New York: New Directions, 1989).

4. Jean-Paul Sartre, *Being and Nothingness: An Essay on Phenomenological Ontology,* trans. Hazel E. Barnes (New York: Philosophical Library, 1956).

5. Sartre, *The Flies,* 118-19 (Act 3).

6. Lewis Carroll, *Alice's Adventures in Wonderland,* in *The Annotated Alice: "Alices's Adventures in Wonderland" and "Through the Looking Glass,"* ed. Martin Gardner (New York: Bramhall House, 1960), 88.

7. Sartre, *Being and Nothingness,* 252-302.

8. Sartre, *No Exit*, 45.

9. Ibid., 46.

CHAPTER 14: DARWIN AND FREUD: INFLUENTIAL THINKERS

1. Charles Darwin, *The Origin of Species*, ed. Gillian Beer, Oxford World's Classics (New York: Oxford University Press, 1998).

2. Charles Lyell, *Principles of Geology*, 3 vols. (1832; reprint New York: Cramer, 1970).

3. Erasmus Darwin, *Zoonomia; or, The Laws of Organic Life*, 2 vols. (Philadelphia: Dobson, 1797).

4. Timothy Ferris, *Coming of Age in the Milky Way* (New York: Morrow, 1988), 236-38.

5. Sigmund Freud, *Totem and Taboo*, trans. James Strachey (Scranton, Pa.: Norton, 1990).

6. Sigmund Freud, *The Future of an Illusion*, ed. James Strachey (Scranton, Pa.: Norton, 1989); Sigmund Freud, *Civilization and Its Discontents*, ed. James Strachey (Scranton, Pa.: Norton, 1989).

CONCLUSION: GILSON'S CHOICE

1. Harvey Cox, *The Secular City: Secularization and Urbanization in Theological Perspective* (New York: Macmillan, 1965).

2. Allan Bloom, *The Closing of the American Mind* (New York: Simon and Schuster, 1987).

3. Dorothy Sayers, *The Lost Tools of Learning: Paper Read at a Vacation Course in Education, Oxford, 1947* (London: Methuen, 1948); reprinted in Anne Husted Burleigh, ed. *Education in a Free Society* (Indianapolis: Liberty Fund, 1973), 145-67.

4. Douglas Wilson, *Recovering the Lost Tools of Learning: An Approach to Distinctively Christian Education* (Wheaton, Ill.: Crossway, 1991).

5. Ludwig Wittgenstein, *Tractatus Logico-philosophicus* (New York: Brace, 1922).

FOR FURTHER READING

Following is a list of philosophy classics mentioned in the book, along with at least one inexpensive edition of each. For current information on Penguin Classics, check the following website:

www.penguinclassics.com

Up-to-date data on Oxford World's Classics are available at the following:

www.worldsclassics.co.uk

The status of titles in the Great Books in Philosophy series and the Great Minds series may be found at this site:

www.prometheusbooks.com

Also included in the list below are relevant portions of standard encyclopedias and histories of philosophy, as well as books by evangelical philosophers, all of which serve as helpful introductions to the philosophers featured in the book. Gordon H. Clark, author of *Thales to Dewey: A History of Philosophy*, was a Reformed thinker whose academic specialty was philosophy.

ARISTOTLE

Aristotle. *The Nicomachean Ethics*. (1) Translated and introduced by David Ross. Translation revised by J. R. Ackrill and J. O. Urmson. Oxford World's Classics. New York: Oxford University, 1998. (2) Great Books in Philosophy. Amherst, N.Y.: Prometheus, n.d.

Clark, Gordon H. *Thales to Dewey: A History of Philosophy*. Boston:

Houghton Mifflin, 1957. Reprint ed. Hobbs, N.M.: Trinity Foundation, 1997. 96-144.

Copleston, Frederick, S.J. *A History of Philosophy.* 9 vols. Westminster, Md.: Newman, 1946–75. Reprint ed. Image Books. New York: Doubleday, 1993. 1:266-378.

Irwin, T. H. "Aristotle." In Edward Craig, ed. *Routledge Encyclopedia of Philosophy.* 10 vols. New York: Routledge, 1998. 1:414-35.

Kerferd, G. B. "Aristotle." In Paul Edwards, ed. *The Encyclopedia of Philosophy.* 8 vols. New York: Macmillan, 1967. 1:151-62.

Stumpf, Samuel. *Socrates to Sartre: A History of Philosophy.* New York: McGraw-Hill, 1966. 85-115.

AUGUSTINE

Augustine. *The City of God.* Edited by David Knowles. Translated by Henry Bettenson. Penguin Classics. New York: Penguin, 1984.

———. *Confessions.* (1) Translated and edited by Henry Chadwick. Oxford World's Classics. New York: Oxford University, 1998. (2) Translated and introduced by R. S. Pine-Coffin. Penguin Classics. Edited by Betty Radice. New York: Penguin, 1961.

Clark, Gordon H. *Thales to Dewey: A History of Philosophy.* Boston: Houghton Mifflin, 1957. Reprint ed. Hobbs, N.M.: Trinity Foundation, 1997. 218-46.

Copleston, Frederick, S.J. *A History of Philosophy.* 9 vols. Westminster, Md.: Newman, 1946–75. Reprint ed. Image Books. New York: Doubleday, 1993. 2:40-90.

Garcia, Janet, ed. *Christian History* 6, 3 (1987). The entire issue (no. 15) of this magazine is devoted to Augustine.

Geisler, Norman. *What Augustine Says.* Grand Rapids, Mich.: Baker, 1982.

Markus, R. A. "Augustine, St." In Paul Edwards, ed. *The Encyclopedia of Philosophy.* 8 vols. New York: Macmillan, 1967. 1:198-207.

Matthews, Gareth B. "Augustine of Hippo." In Edward Craig, ed. *Routledge Encyclopedia of Philosophy.* 10 vols. New York: Routledge, 1998. 1:541-59.

Sproul, R. C., Jr. *Table Talk* (June 1996). Several articles in this issue of Ligonier Ministries' devotional magazine are devoted to Augustine.

Stumpf, Samuel. *Socrates to Sartre: A History of Philosophy.* New York: McGraw-Hill, 1966. 141-59.

CHARLES DARWIN

Darwin, Charles. *The Origin of Species.* (1) Edited by Gillian Beer. Oxford World's Classics. New York: Oxford University, 1998. (2) Great Minds Series. Amherst, N.Y.: Prometheus, 1991. (3) Edited by J. W. Burrow. Penguin Classics. New York: Penguin, 1982.

"Darwin, Charles Robert." In John Daintith et al. *Biographical Encyclopedia of Scientists*. 2d ed. Philadelphia: Institute of Physics, 1994. 1:203-4.

de Beer, Gavin. "Darwin, Charles Robert." In Charles Coulston Gillispie, ed. *Dictionary of Scientific Biography*. 16 vols. New York: Scribner, 1970–80.

RENÉ DESCARTES

Clark, Gordon H. *Thales to Dewey: A History of Philosophy*. Boston: Houghton Mifflin, 1957. Reprint ed. Hobbs, N.M.: Trinity Foundation, 1997. 308-324.

Copleston, Frederick, S.J. *A History of Philosophy*. 9 vols. Westminster, Md.: Newman, 1946–75. Reprint ed. Image Books. New York: Doubleday, 1993. 4:63-152.

Descartes, René. *Discourse on Method and The Meditations*. (1) Translated and introduced by F. E. Sutcliffe. Penguin Classics. New York: Penguin, 1968. (2) Great Books in Philosophy. Amherst, N.Y.: Prometheus, n.d.

———. *Rules for the Direction of the Mind*. Extracts in *Discourse on Method and Related Writings*. Translated and introduced by Desmond M. Clarke. Penguin Classics. New York: Penguin, 1999.

Garber, Daniel. "Descartes, René." In Edward Craig, ed. *Routledge Encyclopedia of Philosophy*. 10 vols. New York: Routledge, 1998. 3:1-19.

Scruton, Roger. *From Descartes to Wittgenstein: A Short History of Modern Philosophy*. Boston: Routledge & Kegan Paul, 1981. 29-39.

Stumpf, Samuel. *Socrates to Sartre: A History of Philosophy*. New York: McGraw-Hill, 1966. 249-61.

Williams, Bernard. "Descartes, René." In Paul Edwards, ed. *The Encyclopedia of Philosophy*. 8 vols. New York: Macmillan, 1967. 2:344-54.

SIGMUND FREUD

Freud, Sigmund. *Civilization and Its Discontents*. Edited by James Strachey. Scranton, Pa.: Norton, 1989.

———. *The Future of an Illusion*. Edited by James Strachey. Scranton, Pa.: Norton, 1989.

———. *Totem and Taboo*. Translated by James Strachey. Scranton, Pa.: Norton, 1990.

"Freud, Sigmund." In Susan Gall, ed. *The Gale Encyclopedia of Psychology*. Detroit: Gale, 1996. 156-58.

Pelzer, K. E. "Freud, Sigmund." In H. J. Eysenck, Wilhelm Arnold, and Richard Meili, eds. *Encyclopedia of Psychology*. 3 vols. London: Search, 1972. 1:388.

Wallace, E. R., IV. "Freud, Sigmund." In David G. Benner and Peter C. Hill, eds. *Baker Encyclopedia of Psychology and Counseling*. 2d ed. Grand Rapids, Mich.: Baker, 1999. 473-76.

DAVID HUME

Baier, Annette. "Hume, David." In Edward Craig, ed. *Routledge Encyclopedia of Philosophy.* 10 vols. New York: Routledge, 1998. 4:543-62.

Clark, Gordon H. *Thales to Dewey: A History of Philosophy.* Boston: Houghton Mifflin, 1957. Reprint ed. Hobbs, N.M.: Trinity Foundation, 1997. 381-94.

Copleston, Frederick, S.J. *A History of Philosophy.* 9 vols. Westminster, Md.: Newman, 1946–75. Reprint ed. Image Books. New York: Doubleday, 1993. 5:258-353.

Hume, David. *Dialogue Concerning Natural Religion.* (1) Edited by J. C. A. Gaskin. Oxford World's Classics. New York: Oxford University, 1998. (2) Edited by Martin Bell. Penguin Classics. New York: Penguin, 1990. (3) Great Books in Philosophy. Amherst, N.Y.: Prometheus, n.d.

————. *An Enquiry Concerning Human Understanding.* Great Books in Philosophy. Amherst, N.Y.: Prometheus, 1988.

————. *Essays Moral, Political, and Literary.* Edited by Eugene F. Miller. Rev. ed. Liberty Classics Series. Indianapolis: Liberty Fund, 1987.

————. *A Treatise of Human Nature.* (1) Edited by Ernest C. Mossner. Penguin Classics. New York: Penguin, 1986. (2) Great Books in Philosophy. Amherst, N.Y.: Prometheus, n.d.

MacNabb, D. G. C. "Hume, David." In Paul Edwards, ed. *The Encyclopedia of Philosophy.* 8 vols. New York: Macmillan, 1967. 4:74-90.

Scruton, Roger. *From Descartes to Wittgenstein: A Short History of Modern Philosophy.* Boston: Routledge & Kegan Paul, 1981. 120-33.

Stumpf, Samuel. *Socrates to Sartre: A History of Philosophy.* New York: McGraw-Hill, 1966. 296-303.

IMMANUEL KANT

Clark, Gordon H. *Thales to Dewey: A History of Philosophy.* Boston: Houghton Mifflin, 1957. Reprint ed. Hobbs, N.M.: Trinity Foundation, 1997. 395-433.

Copleston, Frederick, S. J. *A History of Philosophy.* 9 vols. Westminster, Md.: Newman, 1946–75. Reprint ed. Image Books. New York: Doubleday, 1993. 6:180-392.

Guyer, Paul. "Kant, Immanuel." In Edward Craig, ed. *Routledge Encyclopedia of Philosophy.* 10 vols. New York: Routledge, 1998. 5:177-200.

Kant, Immanuel. *Critique of Pure Reason.* Translated by J. M. Meiklejohn. Great Books in Philosophy. Amherst, N.Y.: Prometheus, 1990.

Scruton, Roger. *From Descartes to Wittgenstein: A Short History of Modern Philosophy.* Boston: Routledge & Kegan Paul, 1981. 137-80.

Stumpf, Samuel. *Socrates to Sartre: A History of Philosophy.* New York: McGraw-Hill, 1966. 305-26.

Walsh, W. H. "Kant, Immanuel." In Paul Edwards, ed. *The Encyclopedia of Philosophy.* 8 vols. New York: Macmillan, 1967. 4:305-24.

SØREN KIERKEGAARD

Clark, Gordon H. *Thales to Dewey: A History of Philosophy.* Boston: Houghton Mifflin, 1957. Reprint ed. Hobbs, N.M.: Trinity Foundation, 1997. 485-92.

Copleston, Frederick, S.J. *A History of Philosophy.* 9 vols. Westminster, Md.: Newman, 1946–75. Reprint ed. Image Books. New York: Doubleday, 1993. 7:335-51.

Evans, C. Stephen. *Faith Beyond Reason: A Kierkegaardian Account.* Grand Rapids, Mich.: Eerdmans, 1998.

Gardiner, Patrick. "Kierkegaard, Søren Aabye." In Edward Craig, ed. *Routledge Encyclopedia of Philosophy.* 10 vols. New York: Routledge, 1998. 5:235-44.

Kierkegaard, Søren. *Attack upon "Christendom."* Translated and introduced by Walter Lowrie. Princeton, N.J.: Princeton University, 1968.

———. *Concluding Unscientific Postscript to "Philosophical Fragments."* Edited and translated by Howard V. Hong and Edna H. Hong. Vol. 1, *Text.* Princeton, N.J.: Princeton University, 1992.

———. *Either/Or.* (1) Unabridged ed. Edited and translated by Howard V. Hong and Edna H. Hong. 2 vols. Princeton, N.J.: Princeton University, 1987. (2) Abridged ed. Translated and edited by Alastair Hannay. Penguin Classics. New York: Penguin, 1992.

———. *Fear and Trembling.* Translated and introduced by Alastair Hannay. Penguin Classics. New York: Penguin, 1986.

MacIntyre, Alasdair. "Kierkegaard, Søren Aabye." In Paul Edwards, ed. *The Encyclopedia of Philosophy.* 8 vols. New York: Macmillan, 1967. 4:336-40.

Scruton, Roger. *From Descartes to Wittgenstein: A Short History of Modern Philosophy.* Boston: Routledge & Kegan Paul, 1981. 186-90.

Stumpf, Samuel. *Socrates to Sartre: A History of Philosophy.* New York: McGraw-Hill, 1966. 455-61.

JOHN LOCKE

Ayers, Michael. "Locke, John." In Edward Craig, ed. *Routledge Encyclopedia of Philosophy.* 10 vols. New York: Routledge, 1998. 5:665-87.

Clapp, James Gordon. "Locke, John." In Paul Edwards, ed. *The Encyclopedia of Philosophy.* 8 vols. New York: Macmillan, 1967. 4:487-503.

Clark, Gordon H. *Thales to Dewey: A History of Philosophy.* Boston: Houghton Mifflin, 1957. Reprint ed. Hobbs, N.M.: Trinity Foundation, 1997. 358-69.

Copleston, Frederick, S.J. *A History of Philosophy.* 9 vols. Westminster, Md.: Newman, 1946–75. Reprint ed. Image Books. New York: Doubleday, 1993. 5:67-142.

Locke, John. *An Essay Concerning Human Understanding.* (1) Edited by Alexander Campbell Fraser. 2 vols. New York: Dover, 1959. (2) Edited by Roger Woolhouse. Penguin Classics. New York: Penguin, 1998.

———. *Two Treatises of Government.* Edited by Peter Laslett. Student ed. *Cambridge Texts in the History of Political Thought.* Edited by Raymond Geuss and Quentin Skinner. Cambridge: Cambridge University Press, 1988.

———. *The Second Treatise on Civil Government.* Great Books in Philosophy. Amherst, N.Y.: Prometheus, 1986.

Scruton, Roger. *From Descartes to Wittgenstein: A Short History of Modern Philosophy.* Boston: Routledge & Kegan Paul, 1981. 85-98.

Stumpf, Samuel. *Socrates to Sartre: A History of Philosophy.* New York: McGraw-Hill, 1966. 279-89.

KARL MARX

Clark, Gordon H. *Thales to Dewey: A History of Philosophy.* Boston: Houghton Mifflin, 1957. Reprint ed. Hobbs, N.M.: Trinity Foundation, 1997. 477-85.

McInnes, Neil. "Marx, Karl." In Paul Edwards, ed. *The Encyclopedia of Philosophy.* 8 vols. New York: Macmillan, 1967. 5:171-73.

Marx, Karl. *Capital.* (1) Unabridged ed. 3 vols. Translated by Ben Fowkes and David Fernbach. Introduced by Ernest Mandel. Penguin Classics. New York: Penguin, 1992–93. (2) Abridged ed. Edited by David McLellan. Oxford World's Classics. New York: Oxford University, 1999.

Rosen, Michael. "Marx, Karl." In Edward Craig, ed. *Routledge Encyclopedia of Philosophy.* 10 vols. New York: Routledge, 1998. 6:118-33.

Scruton, Roger. *From Descartes to Wittgenstein: A Short History of Modern Philosophy.* Boston: Routledge & Kegan Paul, 1981. 212-25.

Stumpf, Samuel. *Socrates to Sartre: A History of Philosophy.* New York: McGraw-Hill, 1966. 421-36.

FRIEDRICH NIETZSCHE

Clark, Gordon H. *Thales to Dewey: A History of Philosophy.* Boston: Houghton Mifflin, 1957. Reprint ed. Hobbs, N.M.: Trinity Foundation, 1997. 492-98.

Clark, Maudamarie. "Nietzsche, Friedrich." In Edward Craig, ed. *Routledge Encyclopedia of Philosophy.* 10 vols. New York: Routledge, 1998. 6:844-61.

Copleston, Frederick, S.J. *A History of Philosophy.* 9 vols. Westminster, Md.: Newman, 1946–75. Reprint ed. Image Books. New York: Doubleday, 1993. 7:390-420.

Kaufmann, Walter. "Nietzsche, Friedrich." In Paul Edwards, ed. *The Encyclopedia of Philosophy*. 8 vols. New York: Macmillan, 1967. 5:504-14.

Nietzsche, Friedrich. *Thus Spake Zarathustra*. (1) Translated and introduced by R. J. Hollingdale. Penguin Classics. New York: Penguin, 1961. (2) Edited by H. James Birx. Great Books in Philosophy. Amherst, N.Y.: Prometheus, 1997. (3) Translated by Walter Kaufmann. New York: The Modern Library, 1995.

Scruton, Roger. *From Descartes to Wittgenstein: A Short History of Modern Philosophy*. Boston: Routledge & Kegan Paul, 1981. 190-94.

Stumpf, Samuel. *Socrates to Sartre: A History of Philosophy*. New York: McGraw-Hill, 1966. 375-85.

PLATO

Clark, Gordon H. *Thales to Dewey: A History of Philosophy*. Boston: Houghton Mifflin, 1957. Reprint ed. Hobbs, N.M.: Trinity Foundation, 1997. 44-95.

Copleston, Frederick, S.J. *A History of Philosophy*. 9 vols. Westminster, Md.: Newman, 1946–75. Reprint ed. Image Books. New York: Doubleday, 1993. 1:127-262.

Plato. *Dialogues*. Edited by Eric H. Warmington and Philip Rouse. Mentor. New York: Penguin, 1956.

———. *Meno*. In *Protagoras and Meno*. Translated and introduced by W. K. C. Guthrie. Penguin Classics. New York: Penguin, 1957.

———. *Phaedo*. Translated by David Gallop. Oxford World's Classics. New York: Oxford University Press, 1999.

———. *The Republic*. (1) Translated by Robin Waterfield. Oxford World's Classics. New York: Oxford University Press, 1998. (2) Translated and introduced by Desmond Lee. Penguin Classics. New York: Penguin, 1955. (3) Great Books in Philosophy. Amherst, N.Y.: Prometheus, n.d.

Ryle, Gilbert. "Plato." In Paul Edwards, ed. *The Encyclopedia of Philosophy*. 8 vols. New York: Macmillan, 1967. 6:314-33.

Schofield, Malcolm. "Plato." In Edward Craig, ed. *Routledge Encyclopedia of Philosophy*. 10 vols. New York: Routledge, 1998. 7:399-421.

Stumpf, Samuel. *Socrates to Sartre: A History of Philosophy*. New York: McGraw-Hill, 1966. 48-84.

JEAN-PAUL SARTRE

Copleston, Frederick, S.J. *A History of Philosophy*. 9 vols. Westminster, Md.: Newman, 1946–75. Reprint ed. Image Books. New York: Doubleday, 1993. 9:340-89.

Howells, Christina. "Sartre, Jean-Paul." In Edward Craig, ed. *Routledge Encyclopedia of Philosophy*. 10 vols. New York: Routledge, 1998. 8:473-79.

Olafson, Frederick A. "Sartre, Jean-Paul." In Paul Edwards, ed. *The Encyclopedia of Philosophy*. 8 vols. New York: Macmillan, 1967. 7:287-93.

Sartre, Jean-Paul. *Being and Nothingness*. Translated and introduced by Hazel E. Barnes. Riverside, N.J.: Pocket Books, 1993.

———. *The Flies*. In *"No Exit" and Three Other Plays*. Translated by Stuart Gilbert. New York: Vintage, 1989. 47-124.

———. *Nausea*. Translated by Lloyd Alexander. Edited by Hayden Carruth. New York: New Directions, 1964.

———. *No Exit*. In *"No Exit" and Three Other Plays*. New York: Vintage, 1989. 1-46.

Scruton, Roger. *From Descartes to Wittgenstein: A Short History of Modern Philosophy*. Boston: Routledge & Kegan Paul, 1981. 264-70.

Stumpf, Samuel. *Socrates to Sartre: A History of Philosophy*. New York: McGraw-Hill, 1966. 465-70.

Thomas Aquinas

Bourke, Vernon J. "Thomas Aquinas, St." In Paul Edwards, ed. *The Encyclopedia of Philosophy*. 8 vols. New York: Macmillan, 1967. 8:105-16.

Clark, Gordon H. *Thales to Dewey: A History of Philosophy*. Boston: Houghton Mifflin, 1957. Reprint ed. Hobbs, N.M.: Trinity Foundation, 1997. 269-84.

Copleston, Frederick, S.J. *A History of Philosophy*. 9 vols. Westminster, Md.: Newman, 1946–75. Reprint ed. Image Books. New York: Doubleday, 1993. 2:302-434.

Kretzmann, Norman. "Aquinas, Thomas." In Edward Craig, ed. *Routledge Encyclopedia of Philosophy*. 10 vols. New York: Routledge, 1998. 1:326-50.

Sproul, R. C., Jr., ed. *Table Talk* (May 1994). Several articles in this issue of Ligonier Ministries' devotional magazine are devoted to Thomas Aquinas.

Stumpf, Samuel. *Socrates to Sartre: A History of Philosophy*. New York: McGraw-Hill, 1966. 185-211.

Thomas Aquinas. *Summa Theologica*. (1) Unabridged ed. 5 vols. Allen, Tex.: Christian Classics, 1981. (2) Abridged ed. Edited by Timothy McDermott. Allen, Tex.: Christian Classics, 1997.

INDEX